NOUN=VERB

By Sosé Gjelaj and Elitsa Teneva

Sosé Gjelaj dedicates Noun=Verb to Adeline.

TABLE OF CONTENTS

INTRODUCTON

Spirituality is at the heart of life. From religion and education to mental health services and the judicial system, the present governments invert spirituality in humanity as a means to overpower life. The goal of the undertaking is the acquisition of absolute corporate profit. Noun=Verb delves deeply into the deceit and methods implemented by the various governing sectors and the derived from such practices alarming outcomes, including psychological disorders, crime, drugs, unemployment and suicide. It presents essential knowledge and practices pertinent to spirituality and calls for the courage to re-embody the sacred energy and prevent the extinction of the human race and life on Earth.

Chapter 1

MYSTICAL REVELATIONS

1.1 Human Being

The human being is "such a complex mystery that neither a single branch of science nor all the sciences together are able to understand him/her fully." The integration of various fields of science will facilitate the understanding of the human being and assist him or her in achieving "lasting fulfilment" and "attending" to his or her "transcendental...and spiritual needs. Far beyond the harm caused by the abuse of religion for selfish interests by many, including its leaders" (Vayalilkarottu, 2012).

1.2 Spirituality

Spirit is beyond language (Corrigan, 2010). The "original Latin word *spiritual*" is defined as "of or pertaining to the spirit or soul as distinguished from the physical nature." Nye (1995, p. 146) further defines spirituality as "awareness sensing...mystery sensing...value sensing." Harris & Moran (1998, p. 109) add that spirituality is "our way of being in the world...in the light of the Mystery at the core of the universe" and Tacey (2000, p. 17) concludes that spirituality represents "a desire for connectedness, which often expresses itself in an emotional relationship with an invisible sacred presence." Spirituality "involves an awareness of interconnectedness with transcendence" and "can be conceived as being outside of the religious traditions" (Mountain, 2007), defined as "the organizational and community structure of the faith traditions that generally include attention to sacred scriptures, a doctrine that outlines the values and beliefs of the faith, and spiritual

2

models to emulate...Between 20 and 35% of Americans consider themselves to be 'spiritual but not religious'" (Plante, 2008).

"Steiner made a clear distinction between unconscious altered states and the stage arrived at through 'disciplined meditative work,' where this 'inner work consists in a heightening, not a lowering of the ordinary consciousness.'" Both Rudolf Steiner and Ken Wilber suggest that "human consciousness is evolving beyond the 'formal,' abstract, intellectual mode towards a 'postformal,' integral mode" where more imaginative, self-reflective, complex, and dialectic ways of loving, living and thinking emerge. While Steiner refers to such state as "consciousness/spiritual soul," Wilber defines it as "vision-logic." According to Steiner, consciousness/spiritual soul is "the highest manifestation of the personal soul, or 'I', beyond which development moves into the more purely spiritual realm" (Gidley, 2007). According to Steiner, "it is simply impossible to prove the existence of spirit to someone else, it is only possible to demonstrate it to oneself, through experience" (Oberski, 2011). According to Carl Jung, "the ultimate goal of the individuation process is the realization of the authentic Self" (McClary, 2007). "The kingdom of God is to be found within" (Dykstra, 2012).

Being spiritual implies being aware of self as spirit and soul, not form and body, thinking and acting from such state of awareness. The majority of humanity is taught to perceive itself solely as a physical form. Such "wrong sense of self...creates all fear, anger and sadness in life...these emotions are always the result of ego (misidentification)," blocking "access to one's true spiritual nature which is peaceful, loving and joyful." In other words, spirituality implies transcending "false identities" (i.e., gender; race; nationality), dissolving ego, becoming virtuous in character and knowing oneself as "love, peace, purity and bliss." In his book, "*Education and Spirituality*," Ramon Gallegos Nava states: "spirituality makes us aware, religion makes us dependent and unconscious" (Chaudhary & Aswal, 2013).

Durkheim (1898) predicts a future spiritual collective realm called the "cult of man" and based upon the values of "personal freedom and civil liberties...a shared collectivity of free individuals, with each developing to their maximum personal potential." Jung echoes Durkheim's vision, reframing it as "going 'only your own way' with no imitation." He adds "mutual love in community" and "an identity with 'the whole of mankind'" as a direct consequence of individuation, also referred to as self-realization, "being as such...the true self that simply and singly is...eternal in each moment." According to Jung, "in solitude your own God leads you to the God of others and...to the Self in others" (Hunt, 2012).

1.2.1 Research

"In recent years every major medical, psychiatric and behavioral medicine journal has published on the topic" of spirituality. "Neurobiological studies prove that...spirituality" is "hardwired into the human brain and human nature...Substantial research evidence shows that spirituality" is "positively associated with happiness and wellbeing" (Vayalilkarottu, 2012).

1.2.2 Education

Imagination and creativity-based activities in education represent one way to facilitate spiritual development (Mountain, 2007).

Discussion

While spirituality is inherently present within human beings, religion is a socially created construct. Whereas spirituality implies identification with love realized from within through a connection with sacred energy, religion denotes servitude to dogma existing outside of oneself or identification with form separate from the sacred source. Hence, religion represents the equivalent of inverted spirituality. The experiences of fear, anger and sadness it invokes are subsequently in exact juxtaposition to the natural emotions of "love, peace, purity and bliss" derived through spirituality. The finding that 20% to 35% of Americans perceive themselves as "spiritual but not religious" indicates that religion is not an essential component of life. Evidence demonstrating a positive association between spirituality and wellbeing implicates that spirituality is.

1.3 Imagination and Creativity

1.3.1 Imagination

Imagination is a constant and natural aspect of being a human (Pelaprat & Cole, 2011), "central to our survival" (Mountain, 2007). "Imagination is the basis of all human activity and an important component of all aspects of cultural life" (Zittoun & Cerchia, 2013). According to Sartre (1972), imagination is "at the very centre of human consciousness;" it "shows the human as 'transcendentally free.' That is, the human stays in the world but the imagination produces the 'unreal' outside of the world." Imagination is at the core of abstract relationships awareness as it allows for the creation of a "picture" which extends beyond the "concrete senses." It is "a bridge which connects unknowns to knowns" (Mountain, 2007).

A working hypothesis suggests that imagination serves the purpose of reconciling the gap between a person's conditional reality and his or her "ongoing flow of thinking" in order to be able to "act and think in the present." Imagination allows us to experience "a better representation of reality" (Zittoun & Cerchia, 2013). As such, imagination is "an advanced human component of identity" (Mountain, 2007), "a form of enrichment, or expansion, of one's experience and understanding of the world" (Zittoun & Cerchia, 2013). Imagination can "process the event, discover new truth, and find a way forward" as part of a distressful experience (Mountain, 2007). It allows for innovation (Foster, 2011), invention, revisiting of the past, exploration of probable futures, consideration of alternatives and expansion of "what is otherwise possible in a given state of socio-historical constraints" (Zittoun & Cerchia, 2013).

1.3.1.1 Personal Identity

A number of philosophers attest to the fact that personal identity is "a created and largely social phenomenon" (Foster, 2011). It is through imagination and experience that the self is created or found." Human beings "are engaged in experimenting with different ways of being." The imagination "is active in these changes" (Mountain, 2007). Imagination, cognition and affective capacity play a vital role in creating self-identity and thus reality. Emotions trigger the imagination which, in combination with cognition, establishes the basis for experiencing reality (Foster, 2011). Feelings derived from imagination "can be systematic in producing behavior" (Braddock, 2011). Various "social selves...first arise" in the "imagination and are then enacted, modified, and finally claimed as part of the core self." Imagination is "deeply involved in making meaning" and is where "faith and hope take root" (Mountain, 2007). According to Sartre, creating a personal identity serves the purpose of realizing our godliness, becoming conscious and complete, merging our subject side or "being-for-itself" with our object aspect or "being-in-itself" (Foster, 2011).

1.3.1.2 Education

"The significance of cultivating the imagination in education has been stressed by numerous educators. Such an enlivening of education may even assist the urgent resuscitation of a dying planetary ecosystem" (Gidley, 2007).

1.3.2 Creativity

"People can use their creative ability to be both moral and immoral" (Yang, 2013). Moral conduct is grounded in character, a "psychological muscle" (Liau et al., 2003).

***

"Imagination is the driving force behind...creativity" (Gundogan & Gonen, 2013). Creativity is "an elusive and complex notion" (Kleiman, 2008), especially challenging to define and to measure (Burnard & White, 2008). Generally, creativity has been defined as "any act, idea, or product that changes an existing domain into [a] new one" (Clegg, 2008) or "the ability to generate ideas and problem solutions that are both novel and appropriate" (Kleibeuker et al., 2013). There are as many various dimensions and kinds of creativity as there are of learning (Claxton, 2006).

Creativity is a life force, "a form and expression of productive energy" (Clegg, 2008), "a cornerstone of human society." Creativity is a "prerequisite for human survival...prosperity" (Kleibeuker et al., 2013) and the evolution of human kind. "Creativity underlies all of human activity" (Geist & Hohn, 2009). "It is precisely human creative activity that makes the human being a creature oriented toward the future, creating the future and thus altering his own present" (Pelaprat & Cole, 2011). Creativity takes place when a new idea or a pattern is discovered and included within a relevant field. A creative person denotes "someone whose thoughts or actions change a domain, or establish a new one." Creative subsequent generations come in contact with such novelty and transform it further (Clegg, 2008).

Creativity plays a vital role in problem solving, critical and analytical thinking (Geist & Hohn, 2009). The analytic, synthetic and practical-contextual intellectual abilities related to creativity have been identified. The analytic ability facilitates discernment between ideas worth pursuing and ideas not worth pursuing. The synthetic ability allows one to view problems from a different perspective and overcome the limitations of conventional thought. The practical-contextual ability serves the function of implementing new ideas and persuasively communicating their value to others (Loia & Dillon, 2006). Divergent and convergent thinking have been further linked to creative cognition (Kleibeuker et al., 2013). Divergent thinking plays a significant role in problem solving and innovation (van den Berg & Hoicka, 2014). Creativity has lastly been associated with working memory and verbal fluency (Kleibeuker et al., 2013) and has been identified as the landmark of intelligence (Geist & Hohn, 2009).

1.3.2.1 Wisdom

A "uniform definition" of wisdom does not exist as "definitions of wisdom are bound by time and by space" (Craft, 2006). According to Hart (2001b, p. 5), "wisdom is distinguished from bare intellect especially by its integration of the heart...We might even think of wisdom as the power of the mind to honor the insights of the heart" (Gidley, 2007). Metacognitive skills have, however, been identified as components of wisdom by the Berlin school and Sternberg's team.

Creativity without wisdom "may not serve children, their families and communities, and the wider social and cultural groupings to which they belong" (Craft, 2006). Anna

Craft (The Open University, UK) adds that creativity and wisdom need to be cultivated in the classroom (Burnard, 2006). It has been suggested that students and teachers will be encouraged to take into consideration the effects of their ideas on themselves and their environment once wisdom becomes an integral part of fostering creativity in the classroom (Craft, 2006).

1.3.2.2 Parental Expectations

According to Bronfenbrenner (2005), obedience, politeness, respecting authority and parental wishes, diligence, appropriate behavior, setting and achieving long-term goals, are parental expectations that could cultivate self-discipline in children, yet could also impede the development of problem-solving skills, creativity and critical thinking (Leu, 2008).

1.3.2.3 Education

All children are born with potential for creativity. The years between three years of age and five are critical for the development of creativity (ZachopoulUoa et al., 2006). According to Gardner (1982), the preschool years are "a golden age of creativity, a time when every child sparkles with artistry" (Coates & Coates, 2006). The founder of the kindergarten, Friedrich Froebel, believed first and foremost that "education must nurture creativity."

Systematic and meaningful research in the field of creativity is scarce despite the fact that the "creative child" has been the focus of early childhood education in the United States. It is an irony that early childhood education which views creativity as the core element of education has generated scarce creativity research while scholars studying creativity have largely dismissed educational goals and means (Feldman & Benjamin, 2006). Research findings

9

demonstrated that highly creative children had the lowest chance of academic success. Such children were challenged by meeting deadlines, course outcomes and examination board requirements. Study results further revealed that "assessment strategies inhibit student creativity" (Simmons & Thompson, 2008).

It is believed by many that creativity will weaken if the necessary conditions for its continual expression are not set in place (Feldman & Benjamin, 2006). To "show its power," creativity must "be free from all ideologies that have the potential to constrain or oppress" (Clegg, 2008). It is unfortunate that the majority of children "learn to conform" to what is expected of them rather than "fight to retain their creativity and be a school 'outsider'" (Geist & Hohn, 2009). Acting on creativity requires "the ability to take intellectual risks, and to recognize and overcome constraints" (Clegg, 2008).

Though there is a need to explicitly delineate what constitutes creative teaching and what its effects are on creative learning (Burnard & White, 2008), "creative teachers and creative teaching" have been recognized as "key components in fostering creativity in young children" (Zachopouloua et al., 2006). According to Epstein (2008), fostering creativity could enhance children's academic performance and learning processes and "encourage lifelong learning" (Geist & Hohn, 2009). Many academics hold the opinion that teachers' ability to establish an optimal learning environment for children and to interact with them is essential to encouraging "children's use of creative and critical thinking skills." Teachers can foster creativity in the classroom by modeling creativity, asking open-ended questions and "encouraging experimentation" (Zachopouloua et al., 2006). According to Gordon, active listening and open-ended questions encourage children to interact with teachers and contributes to a "child's creative and active mind to develop" (Geist & Hohn, 2009). An educational curriculum that utilizes modalities such as kinesthetic exploration, problem solving, self-expression and discovery could enhance children's creative thinking abilities. According to Torrance (1981), kinesthetic activities are most suitable to withdraw creativity in the preschool years. Researchers have demonstrated that motor creativity is directly correlated to critical and creative thinking. Capel (1986) adds that movement allows children to "develop their inventiveness, creativity, and their spirit of adventure" (Zachopouloua et al., 2006). Daria Loi (RMIT University, Australia) and Patrick Dillon (Exeter University, UK) add pedagogical and technological implementation of analysis, synthesis and transference within educational settings as a further means to fostering creativity (Burnard, 2006). It has been finally demonstrated that short and long-term meditation fosters and enhances creativity (Ding et al., 2014). A number of reports propose that "rest/relaxation, meditation, sleep, and dreams are a major source of creative ideas" (Haier & Jung, 2008). According to neo-Platonism and Gnosticism, "contemplative meditation is *both* a higher individual ascent of the soul *and* a reminiscence, a return to origins that travels up the path of descent from a divine creation" (Hunt, 2012).

***

Boldness is required to challenge the "sometimes oppressive ideologies and organizational structures that stifle and contain our creative selves." A critical scholar who desires to foster student creativity must operate within a "permanent framework of ambiguity" confined by "bureaucratic rules, academic conventions, the demands of external agencies, and a confusion of conflicting ideologies," on one hand, and devotion to education that aims to liberate students' minds from "outmoded habits of thinking" and from "the edicts of the World Bank or any other organization," on the other

(Clegg, 2008). Within the context of fostering creativity for children, Piitto (2004) proposes that "developing trust is imperative if people are to take risks...and be transformed." There is a greater likelihood for teachers to enhance creativity in their prospective educational settings if they are to collaborate to build "group trust." Support needs to be provided to teachers to "take risks and to work outside the safe, the known and the predictable." Pedagogical autonomy, collaboration between teachers and schools and professional agency are further proposed as essential to encouraging creativity in education factors (Burnard & White, 2008).

Discussion

Imagination is an innate attribute capable of serving two fundamental functions – assisting in the realization of oneself as a spiritual being or experiencing oneself as unauthentic. Alternatively stated, human beings possess the free will and inner power to create their personal realities through engaging the imagination.

1.4 Arts

Children's cognitive ability develops once encouraged to be creative and take joy in the field of arts (Geist & Hohn, 2009). "Evidence is now emerging that shows that arts education can have powerful effects on student achievement," particularly for struggling students (Rabkin & Redmond, 2006). In 1992, the National Assessment of Educational Progress reveled that children performed better academically when their participation in arts classes was more frequent (Geist & Hohn, 2009). Researchers also analyzed the "massive" National Education Longitudinal Study of 1988 database and demonstrated "a significant correlation, growing over time, between arts participation and academic performance. Gains...were greatest for students in the lowest-socioeconomic-status quartile, those most at risk of academic failure."

Additional data suggests that academic curriculum integrating the arts is correlated with greater academic achievement and higher standardized test scores relative to more traditional arts education programs. In comparison to community service and sports programs, a longitudinal study, published in 1999, demonstrated that low-income, higher-risk students preferred and "had far greater academic and developmental benefits" from after-school arts-based programs. A study published in 2003 further revealed that an arts-integrated program in Minneapolis, Minnesota, "had the greatest effect on disadvantaged learners." Many of the students in these programs "went from being withdrawn or disruptive to becoming active and productive class members." Catterall and Waldorf (1999) conducted a study comparing the standardized test scores of 23 arts-integrated schools in Chicago, Illinois, with the scores of students in mainstream schools and showed that the standardized test scores of students in the arts-integrated schools "rose as much as two times faster than the scores of youth in more traditional schools." Upon a thorough review of arts-based teaching and learning within the school environment, Rooney (2004) lastly concluded that arts seemed to enhance students' motivation, cognition, interest, creativity, self-esteem, communication skills and academic performance. Music, drama and visual arts were found to be "useful" in increasing students' literacy skills and cognitive development. "These studies have been ignored in mainstream education" (Rabkin & Redmond, 2006).

It is important that teachers possess the ability to develop creative school activities. Yet, most teachers are not equipped with "significant background in the arts," preventing them from being proficient in arts (Geist & Hohn, 2009).

1.4.1 Drawing

"There is a strong association between a learner's positive emotions and effective learning." Children enjoy "making marks on paper." Drawing is a means of expression and communication. It promotes children's language and literacy development, knowledge construction and motivation to learn. Children become more engaged and expressive during the process of concept acquisition when adults listen to children's explanation of their drawing projects (Chang, 2012).

1.4.2 Music

"We cannot afford to allow a proven educational experience to be used as a political instrument or to be labeled, as it has sadly been in some arenas, as a frivolous luxury. Music education is not only for the wealthier schools; it is fit for all schools. We must promote, explain, and act to get music to all our students" (Petress, 2005).

***

"Music is universal and generally highly valued in human societies. These attributes are biologically grounded in the phylogenetically ancient neural machinery of emotion, reward and memory" (Clark et al., 2014). Albert Einstein viewed music as an "extension of his thinking process, a method of allowing the subconscious to solve difficult problems" (Geist & Hohn, 2009). According to Langer (1957), "music conveys a meaning that cannot be conveyed through language, enabling us to present and to re-present inner deep and powerful feelings" (Lim & Chung, 2008). "Young children reliably identify emotions expressed in music" (Clark et al., 2014). The goal of music instruction is to familiarize children with the symbolical system of music so they can acquire the necessary skills to use "music as a vehicle for giving voice to the inner life of feeling - to 'express the inexpressible'" (Lim & Chung, 2008).

Research demonstrated that music is associated with "cognitive development and learning." Music has been found to correlate with spatial-temporal reasoning, a crucial component to the development of skills in mathematics (Geist & Hohn, 2009). Blanchard (1979) further revealed that playing background music during examination resulted in lower blood pressure and higher exam performance. Different studies shpwed that playing slow rhythms leads to "a more relaxed physiological state" and slower heart rate. These and related research findings "lay the foundation for a connection between music, relaxation, improved brain function, and increased academic performance" (Carlson, 2004).

Discussion

There is a "strong association between a learner's positive emotions and effective learning" (*Drawing, 1.4.1*). Creativity has been described as "the landmark of intelligence" (*Creativity, 1.3.2*). "Children's cognitive ability develops once encouraged to be creative and take joy in the field of arts." Results from studies demonstrated academic improvement once arts (i.e., background music), arts education or arts-integrated programs are introduced as part of the curriculum. Alongside the fact that "systematic and meaningful research in the field of creativity is scarce" (*Education, 1.3.2.3*), "these studies have been ignored in mainstream education." At the same time, "most teachers are not equipped with 'significant background in the arts,'" compromising their ability to develop arts-related "creative school activities." Academic achievement derived through positive emotions-evoking evidence-based practices is therefore not a primary goal of mainstream education.

Furthermore, the finding that music education is prevalent in wealthier schools implies not only that spirituality is a "luxury" within the confines of mainstream education, but also that students from wealthier backgrounds have an economic advantage compared to students of lower socio-economic status (i.e., arts-based educational curriculum improves cognitive skills and academic performance). The reason why public education is conductive to the implementation of music programs solely at affluent schools is questionable.

1.5 Play

Children learn and develop through play (Johnson et al., 1980). Play encourages autonomy (Zhao, 2014) and contributes to the development of motor, cognitive, self-reflective skills and abilities (Zachopouloua et al., 2006), physical, communicative and social development. "Defined this way, play becomes a means to holistic development" (Andang'O & Mugo, 2007). Froebel further viewed play as the educational means through which children's creativity is expressed. Within the context of such view, all children are gifted with creativity (Feldman & Benjamin, 2006).

1.6 Motivation

Fostering autonomy "should be one of the main aims of early childhood education provision" (Zhao, 2014).

***

Motivation has an impact on students' optimism and scholarly achievement. There are 3 general types of motivation – intrinsic, extrinsic and amotivation (Rajiah & Saravanan, 2014). "Intrinsic motivation is viewed as the prototype of autonomy" (Taylor et al., 2014). The Longman

Dictionary of Contemporary English (2011) defines autonomy as "the ability or opportunity to make your own decisions without being controlled by anyone else" (Zhao, 2014). A sense of personal choice and decision are the driving force of autonomous actions (i.e., internal locus of causality) (Taylor et al., 2014). "Human autonomy plays a pivotal role in self-regulation and performance. Whatever the behavioral domain, feelings of engagement, diligence, and vitality are higher when the motivation underlying a goal or behavior is autonomous or self-endorsed rather than pressured or controlled" (Legault & Inzlicht, 2013). Intrinsically-motivated individuals "perceive themselves as the causal agents of their own behavior" and undertake a particular activity "simply for the enjoyment and excitement it brings, rather to get a reward or to satisfy a constraint" (Taylor et al., 2014). Self-determination theory postulates that autonomy, relatedness and competence are at the core of learning, psychological well-being and constructive classroom functioning (Cheon & Reeve, 2015). Children's cognitive ability develops once encouraged to be autonomous thinkers and rely on themselves (Geist & Hohn, 2009). Study findings demonstrated that "intrinsic motivation is consistently the most beneficial form of motivation for students' achievement."

In contrast to the autonomous form of intentional action, internal and external pressure factors initiate controlled actions (i.e., external locus of causality) as part of the controlled form of intentional action. Extrinsically-motivated individuals do not engage in an activity resulting out of personal interest, but rather "for the consequence it is thought to be instrumentally linked to" (Taylor et al., 2014).

Lastly, amotivation "is a state of motivational apathy in which students harbor little or no reason (motive) to invest the energy and effort that is necessary to learn or to accomplish something." Lack of interest, perceived low abilities, lack of willingness to put forward required effort and low value placed on the particular subject have been identified as causes of amotivation. Sleeping during class, skipping class, being passive in class (i.e., "I don't see why I should have to participate in class") or acting as if the student is participating (i.e., "I go to school, but I don't know why"), result from amotivation. Amotivation within the educational setting is associated with negative academic outcomes such as school drop-out and low academic performance. Lack of attendance to students' psychological needs (i.e., autonomy; competence) "generates immediate negative affect (e.g., anger, anxiety)" and amotivation. Teachers' controlling nature, failure to take their students' perspectives into consideration, use of intimidation strategies, asserting power, yelling, "pressure and coerce students into compliance," intrude and attempt to change students' behaviors and personal believes, are mainly associated with "students' need frustration." The "classroom antidote to amotivation is for teachers to offer a motivating style capable of involving, vitalizing, and satisfying students' psychological needs" (Cheon & Reeve, 2015).

Discussion

The prototype of a "future spiritual collective realm" consists of "free individuals...going 'only...own way' with no imitation" and "developing to...maximum personal potential" (*Spirituality, 1.2*). If autonomy is an essential condition for the emergence of spirituality while "intrinsic motivation is viewed as the prototype of autonomy," it follows that intrinsic motivation is at the heart of spirituality. Such conclusion is validated by the fact that both intrinsic motivation and spirituality result in the experience of positive affect. The recommendation that a scholar who wishes to foster students' creativity must do so within the confines of bureaucracy, academic conventions, external demands and confusion emanating from conflicting ideologies (*Education, 1.3.2.3*), indicates that the educational system is not conductive to intrinsically motivated action.

1.7 Emotions

"Emotional experiences can be described as socially constructed, personally enacted ways of being that emerge from conscious and/or unconscious judgments regarding perceived successes at attaining goals or maintaining standards or beliefs during transactions as part of social–historical contexts." Positive emotions usually occur when a particular situation invokes an experience of pleasure. Fulfillment and happiness, for example, are experienced when an individual makes goal-oriented progress. Negative emotions, including anger and frustration, are withdrawn "from sources related to goal incongruence" (Timoštšuk & Ugaste, 2012).

Adults may be in a position of punishing children's experiences and emotional expression or disregarding "the world of emotions." Children of parents who dismiss or diminish their emotions may be more fearful, passive and sadder, incapable of optimal emotion regulation. Such children are "likely to suppress showing feelings, but remain physiologically aroused, without skills to rectify the situation or their emotional response." Parents' angry response to children's emotional expression of anger or sadness or happy response to children's sadness "hampers learning about emotions." In contrast, children whose parents encourage expression of emotions "have more access to their own emotions" and are more comprehensive of emotions.

Researchers found that teachers who were unaware of their own emotions were more likely to minimize or disregard children's emotions while teachers' own experience of negative emotions was correlated to such teachers punishing children's emotions (Denham et al.,

2012). Anxiety has been found to be the most prevalent emotion experienced by teachers (Timoštšuk & Ugaste, 2012). Mindfulness, stress management, direct instruction and reflective supervision are strategies designed to promote teacher's emotional aptitude (Denham et al., 2012).

Discussion

"Positive emotions usually occur when a particular situation invokes an experience of pleasure" while spirituality results in "love, peace, purity and bliss" (*Spirituality, 1.2*). Therefore, experiences of pleasure are the equivalent of spirituality when the pleasure is love, bliss, peace and purity-based.

Moreover, research demonstrated that teachers' emotional state is directly projected onto students. Through generalization to the larger population, it could be concluded that each individual is consciously and/or unconsciously engaged in creative activities intended to establish an external reality synchronized with inner emotional experiences.

Last, but not least, it is logical to conclude that "parents' angry response to children's emotional expression of anger or sadness…, 'hampers learning about emotions.'" *Spirituality* (*1.2.*) revealed that being spiritual implies "awareness sensing" and "value sensing." Children would have the opportunity to sense that feelings of sadness or anger are not an expression of their authentic selves once permitted to experience them. Such realization would subsequently allow children to adjust their emotional responses in a way that corresponds to their authentic selves. Prohibiting processing of uncomfortable emotions could hence prevent children from embodying spirituality and experiencing happiness and fulfillment.

1.8 Positive Mood

A meta-analysis based upon 102 studies found that participants in a positive mood exhibited greater creativity on fun and enjoyable creativity tasks compared to participants in a negative mood. Though no significant effect size was found, participants in a negative mood exhibited a tendency towards greater creativity on performance-based or serious creativity tasks compared to participants in a positive mood (Baas et al., 2008).

Selective attention is defined as "the ability to focus on a relevant target and inhibit irrelevant information to facilitate the production of an appropriate response." According to Easterbrook's broaden-and-build theory, while positive emotions expand the scope of attention, negative emotions limit it (Finucane, 2011).

Discussion

Findings from the meta-analysis demonstrated that positive feelings tend to lead to creative activities furthering the experience of positive emotions. Negative mood, on the other hand, was found to be largely associated with engagement in "performance-based or serious creativity tasks" that, by implication, do not result in the experience of positive affect. Thus, a loop is created wherein and in general terms, feelings drive the direction of the creative action, which withdraws a resonating to the initial affective experience emotional response.

Further, results from the study provide additional support for the inclination of human beings to directly project inner emotional experiences onto the surrounding environment. Yet, the non-statistically significant association between negative mood and serious and performance-based tasks confirms the fact that individuals also possess the free will to shift their focus of attention and create a reality with the potential to evoke experiences different from their inner emotional state.

Last, but not least, "creativity plays a vital role in problem solving" (*Creativity, 1.3.2*) and while "positive emotions expand the scope of attention, negative emotions limit it." Hence, positive feelings assist in problem solving while negative affect limits such opportunity.

1.9 Humor and Laughter

"Humor is an essential part of our daily lives and an important means to cope with stressful life events" (Stieger et al., 2011). "Laughter... is a pervasive non-verbal expression of emotion, which is universally recognized" (Scott et al., 2014). "Humor and laughter can positively influence mood, promote optimism and lead to a change of perspective" (Falkenberg et al., 2011).

Discussion

Aside from play and arts, due to their capacity to withdraw innate positive experiences, humor and laughter represent two additional means through which spirituality is embodied. The "strong association between a learner's positive emotions and effective learning" (*Drawing, 1.4.1*) implies that humor and laughter are also associated with optimal learning.

1.10 Physical Activity

Researchers have demonstrated that physical exercise leads to improvements in memory and learning in humans (Hopkins & Bucci, 2010). Zaichkowsky et al. (1980) proposed that movement contributes to the development of motor, social, cognitive and self-reflective skills and abilities (Zachopouloua et al., 2006). An association has been established between physical activity, mental and physical disorders. "Ample evidence" suggests that physical activity is linked to decreased incidence of breast and colon cancer, cardiovascular disease, Alzheimer's disease, obesity, depression and anxiety (Meeusen, 2014).

Discussion

Alike arts, play, humor and laughter, physical activity contributes to the embodiment of spirituality and improved learning.

1.11 Language Development

Thinking and speaking are related as we can express our thoughts through speech. Children's speech develops in a speech-based environment (Lang, 2003). Researchers have demonstrated that children's "healthy language development" is associated with their interactive and partner-based communication with adults (Chang, 2012). A child develops appropriate and clear speech when he or she "perceives warmth of soul and language from the adults" (Lang, 2003). Children are instructed to repress their speech when routinely conversing with significant others, possibly leading to "no longer consciously knowing their deepest desires and truths" as speech serves as a medium to uncover one's thoughts. Edgar proposed to "speak what we feel, not what we ought to say" (Dykstra, 2012).

Discussion

Similarly to parental and teachers' dismissal, disregard or punishment of children's emotional expression resulting in compromised emotional awareness, regulation and ultimately spiritual development (*Emotions, 1.7*), repressing children's speech leads to children "no longer consciously knowing their deepest desires and truths." Alternatively stated, suppressing the expression of the innate components comprising human nature (i.e., emotions; thoughts) prevents the unfoldment of spirituality or life.

1.12 Learning and Classroom Environment

The classroom environment (i.e., physical classroom features; motivational climate; interpersonal relationships) has a great impact on students – it can either promote or hinder their learning and value placed on learning, academic achievement and enjoyment (Putwain & Remedios, 2014). A "brain-compatible" classroom setting fosters the connection between learning and the experience of positive emotions.

Ultimately, educators only facilitate what children are inclined to learn in the classroom. "Children's brains need to be immersed in real life, hands on, and meaningful learning experiences" (Rushton, 2011). According to authors such as James Moffett and Ivan Illich, "in a democratic, information-rich society, learning should take place everywhere in the community, and young people should have access to mentors who nourish their diverse personal interests and styles of learning" (Miller).

The *C-space* is a specific type of classroom, described by both staff members and students as a "positive experience in an informal environment." It is perceived as a welcoming and comfortable space that is "conductive of learning" and does not evoke a feeling of a classroom setting. Creative thinking, problem solving, authentic comments and discussions, opportunities for interaction and team-work highlight the atmosphere. The gap between students and lecturers is replaced by a feeling of a "common, shared direction." The *C-space* allows for the accommodation of a range of teaching and learning styles. "It is known that the more comfortable one feels the more likely they are to respond and think creatively" (Jankowska & Atlay, 2008).

Discussion

The "strong association between a learner's positive emotions and effective learning" (*Drawing, 1.4.1*) is reiterated herein.

References

Andang'o, E. & Mugo, J. (2007). Early childhood music education in Kenya: Between broad national policies and local realities. *Arts Education Policy Review*, *109*(2), 43-52.

Baas, M., De Dreu, C. K. & Nijstad, B. A. (2008). A meta-analysis of 25 years of mood-creativity research: Hedonic tone, activation, or regulatory focus? *Psychological Bulletin*, *134*(6), 779-806.

Braddock, L. (2011). Psychological identification, imagination and psychoanalysis. *Philosophical Psychology*, *24*(5), 639-657.

Burnard, P. & White, J. (2008). Creativity and performativity: Counterpoints in British and Australian education. *British Educational Research Journal*, *34*(5), 667-682.

Carlson, J. K., Hoffman, J., Gray, D. & Thompson, A. (2004). A musical interlude: Using music and relaxation to improve reading performance. *Intervention in School and Clinic*, *39*(4), 246-250.

Chang, N. (2012). The role of drawing in young children's construction of science concepts. *Early Childhood Education Journal*, *40*, 187-193.

Chaudhary, B. & Aswal, M. (2013). Imparting spiritual intelligence curriculum in our classrooms. *European Academic Research*, *1*(7), 1508-1515.

Cheon, S. H. & Reeve, J. (2015). A classroom-based intervention to help teachers decrease students' amotivation. *Contemporary Educational Psychology*, *40*, 99-111.

Clark, C. N., Downey, L. E. & Warren, J. D. (2014). Brain disorders and the biological role of music. *Social Cognitive and Affective Neuroscience*, 1-9.

Claxton, G. (2006). Thinking at the edge: Developing soft creativity. *Cambridge Journal of Education*, *36*(3), 351-362.

Clegg, P. (2008). Creativity and critical thinking in the globalised university. *Innovations in Education and Teaching International*, *45*(3), 219-226.

Coates, E. & Coates, A. (2006). Young children talking and drawing. *International Journal of Early Years Education*, *14*(3), 221-241.

Corrigan, P. T. (2010). Spirituality and literary studies. *ENCOUNTER: Education for Meaning and Social Justice*, *23*(4), 47-51.

Craft, A. (2006). Fostering creativity with wisdom. *Cambridge Journal of Education*, *36*(3), 337-350.

Denham, S. A., Bassett, H. H. & Zinsser, K. (2012). Early childhood teachers as socializers of young children's emotional competence. *Early Childhood Education Journal*, *40*, 137-143.

Ding, X., Tang, Y.-Y., Tang, R. & Posner, M. I. (2014). Improving creativity performance by short-term meditation. *Behavioral and Brain Functions*, *10*(9), 1-8.

Dykstra, R. C. (2012). Unrepressing the kingdom: Pastoral theology as aesthetic imagination, *Pastoral Psychology*, *61*, 391-409.

Falkenberg, I., Buchkremer, G., Bartels, M. & Wild, B. (2011). Implementation of a manual-based training of humor abilities in patients with depression: A pilot study. *Psychiatry Research*, *186*, 454-457.

Feldman, D. H. & Benjamin, A. C. (2006). Creativity and education: An American retrospective. *Cambridge Journal of Education*, *36*(3), 319-336.

Foster, G. (2011). Overcoming a Euthyphro problem in personal love: Imagination and personal identity. *Philosophical Psychology*, *24*(6), 825-844.

Finucane, A. M. (2011). The effect of fear and anger on selective attention. *Emotion*, *11*(4), 970-974.

Geist, E. & Hohn, J. (2009). Encouraging creativity in the face of administrative convenience: How our schools discourage divergent thinking. *Education*, *130*(1),141-150.

Gidley, J. M. (2007). Educational imperatives of the evolution of consciousness: The integral visions of Rudolf Steiner and Ken Wilber. *The International Journal of Children's Spirituality*, *12*(2), 117-135.

Gundogan, A., Ari, M. & Gonen, M. (2013). Test of creative imagination: Validity and reliability study. *Educational Sciences: Theory & Practice*, *13*(1), 15-20.

Haier, R. J. & Jung, R. E. (2008). Brain imaging studies of intelligence and creativity: What is the picture for education? *Roeper Review*, *30*, 171-180.

Hopkins, M. E. & Bucci, D. J. (2010). Interpreting the effects of exercise on fear conditioning: The influence of time of day. *Behavioral Neuroscience*, *124*(6), 868-872.

Hunt, H. T. (2012). A collective unconscious reconsidered: Jung's archetypal imagination in the light of contemporary psychology and social science. *Journal of Analytical Psychology*, *57*, 76-98.

Jankowska, M. & Atlay, M. (2008). Use of creative space in enhancing students' engagement. *Innovations in Education and Teaching International*, *45*(3), 271-279.

Johnson, J. E., Ershler, J. & Bell, C. (1980). Play behavior in a discovery-based and a formal-education preschool program. *Child Development*, *51*, 271-274.

Kleibeuker, S. W., De Dreu, C. K. W. & Crone, E. A. (2013). The development of creative cognition across adolescence: Distinct trajectories for insight and divergent thinking. *Developmental Science*, *16*(1), 2-12.

Kleiman, P. (2008). Towards transformation: Conceptions of creativity in higher education. *Innovations in Education and Teaching International, 45*(3), 209-217.

Lang, P. (2003). The kindergarten child. *Association of Waldorf Schools of North America,* 13-16.

Legault, L. & Inzlicht, M. (2013). Self-determination, self-regulation, and the brain: Autonomy improves performance by enhancing neuroaffective responsiveness to self-regulation failure. *Journal of Personality and Social Psychology, 105*(1), 123- 138.

Leu, J. C.-Y. (2008). Early childhood music education in Taiwan: An ecological systems perspective. *Arts Education Policy Review, 109*(3), 17-26.

Liau, A. K., Liau, A. W., Teoh, G. B. S. & Liai, M. T. L. (2003). The case for emotional literacy: The influence of emotional intelligence on problem behaviours in Malaysian secondary school students. *Journal of Moral Education, 32*(1), 51-66.

Lim, N.-H. & Chung, S. (2008). Enriching the context for musical learning. *Arts Education Policy Review, 109*(3), 27-35.

Loia, D. & Dillon, P. (2006). Adaptive educational environments as creative spaces. *Cambridge Journal of Education, 36*(3), 363-381.

McClary, R. (2007). Healing the psyche through music, myth, and ritual. *Psychology of Aesthetics, Creativity, and the Arts, 1*(3), 155-159.

Meeusen, R. (2014). Exercise, nutrition and the brain. *Sports Med, 44*(1), 47-56.

Miller, R. A brief history of alternative education. Retrieved from http://southerncrossreview.org/55/miller-education.htm

Mountain, V. (2007). Educational contexts for the development of children's spirituality: Exploring the use of imagination. *International Journal of Children's Spirituality, 12*(2), 191-205.

Oberski, I. (2011). Rudolf Steiner's philosophy of freedom as a basis for spiritual education? *International Journal of Children's Spirituality*, *16*(1), 5-17.

Pelaprat, E. & Cole, M. (2011). "Minding the Gap:" Imagination, creativity and human cognition. *Integrative Psychological & Behavioral Science*, *45*, 97-418.

Petress, K. (2005). The importance of music education. *Education*, *126*(1), 112-115.

Plante, T. (2008). What do the spiritual and religious traditions offer the practicing psychologist? *Pastoral Psychology*, *56*(4), 429-444.

Putwain, D. & Remedios, R. (2014). The scare tactic: Do fear appeals predict motivation and exam scores? *School Psychology Quarterly*, *29*(4), 503-516.

Rabkin, N. & Redmond, R. (2006). The arts make a difference. *Helping Struggling Students*, *63*(5), 60-64.

Rajiah, K. & Saravanan, C. (2014). The effectiveness of psychoeducation and systematic desensitization to reduce test anxiety among first-year pharmacy students. *American Journal of Pharmaceutical Education*, *78*(9), 1-7.

Rushton, S. (2011). Neuroscience, early childhood education and play: We are doing it right! *Early Childhood Education Journal*, *39*, 89-94.

Scott, S. K., Lavan, N., Chen, S. & McGettigan, C. (2014). The social life of laughter. *Trends in Cognitive Sciences*, *18*(12), 618-620.

Stieger, S., Formann, A. K. & Burger, C. (2011). Humor styles and their relationship to explicit and implicit self-esteem. *Personality and Individual Differences*, *50*, 747-750.

Simmons, R. & Thompson, R. (2008). Creativity and performativity: The case of further education. *British Educational Research Journal*, *34*(5), 601-618.

Taylor, G., Jungert, T., Mageau, G. A., Schattke, K., Dedic, H., Rosenfield. S. & Koestner, R. (2014). A self-determination theory approach to predicting school achievement over time: The unique role of intrinsic motivation. *Contemporary Educational Psychology*, *39*, 342–358.

Timoštšuk, I. & Ugaste, A. (2012). The role of emotions in student teachers' professional identity. *European Journal of Teacher Education*, *35*(4), 421-433.

van den Berg, S. B. & Hoicka, E. (2014). Individual differences and age-related changes in divergent thinking in toddlers and preschoolers. *Developmental Psychology*, *50*(6), 1629-1639.

Vayalilkarottu, J. (2012). Holistic health and well-being: A psycho-spiritual/religious and theological perspective. *Asian Journal of Psychiatry*, *5*, 347-350.

Yang, J. (2013). Linking proactive personality to moral imagination: Moral identity as a moderator. *Social Behavior and Personality*, *41*(3), 165-176.

Zachopouloua, E., Trevlasa, E., Konstadinidoub, E. & Archimedes Project Research Group (2006). The design and implementation of a physical education program to promote children's creativity in the early years. *International Journal of Early Years Education*, *14*(3), 279-294.

Zhao, Y. (2014). Autonomous development in early childhood. *He Kupu*, *5*, 4-10.

Zittoun, T. & Cerchia, F. (2013). Imagination as expansion of experience. *Integrative Psychological & Behavioral Science*, *47*, 305-324.

Chapter 2

MAINSTREAM EDUCATION

"The meaning of words is fluid and can be changed to suit an ideological agenda" (Clegg, 2008). "Governments have agendas" (Horsley, 2009). The neuro-functional aspects of the human brain are thought to have been shaped by biological and social "pressures" (Zaidell, 2014). Jung (1934) believed that the collective unconscious is embedded within "common brain patterns" shared amongst humanity (Hunt, 2012). Under fascist regime, people renounce their own democratic rights in the name of "a leader who they are induced to accept as theirs" (Braddock, 2011).

2.1 Historical Background

Introduced in the 1830's, the aim of the U.S. public education was to "provide a common, culturally unifying educational experience for all children." According to public education historians, between the late 1830s and the early twentieth century, "a particularly narrow model of schooling became solidly established as the 'one best system' of public education. According to this model, the purpose of schooling was to overcome cultural diversity and personal uniqueness in order to mold a loyal citizenry and an effective workforce for the growing industrial system. Education aimed primarily to discipline the developing energies of young people for the sake of political and social uniformity as well as the success of the emerging corporate economy" (Miller).

For approximately half a century, policies in education have contributed to "shaping and linking educational achievement levels with economic development and international competitiveness." (Burnard & White, 2008). In 1983, President Reagan's Commission on Excellence in

Education published "Nation at Risk," a report which made a "powerful statement of the traditional goals of American public schooling–social efficiency and economic growth." Bill Clinton's program enacted into law, "Goals 2000," and George Bush's "America 2000," "continued this top-down movement to harness the young generation's energies to the needs of the corporate economy (Miller).

Internationally, education "is now seen as a commodity" and knowledge - as the means to "create the professionals required by society" (Allam, 2008). Global financial institutions (i.e., the World Bank; the International Monetary Fund) endorse market capitalism and neoliberalism (i.e., marketization; privatization; deregulation) as the basic principles underlying societal governance. Such principles constitute the foundation of the "'reform agenda' promoted by the World Bank for higher education" for a number of years. The goal appears to be the transformation of "academic life" to suit the "neo-liberal economic agenda" (Clegg, 2008).

According to Nixon, the not-for-profit sector, and more specifically, universities, have "become dominated" by a language of productivity, auditing, cost-efficiency, delivery of outcomes and "value for money," to name a few. "Robust evidence" demonstrated that "human capital is a key determinant of economic growth...Investment in human capital and, by implication, higher education has moved to the centre stage of strategies to promote economic prosperity." According to the 2010 edition of *Education at a Glance*, "public resources invested in education ultimately receive returns in even greater tax revenues" (Pouris & Inglesi-Lotz, 2014). Academics, researchers and teachers are "increasingly encouraged...to think in business terms." Such language "fails to recognize the rich unpredictability of learning." It is expected that knowledge will rapidly be transformed into a commodity and education – into training if university settings are consumed by "managerialisation and consumerization" (Clegg, 2008).

Bob Jeffrey (The Open University, UK) stresses the "importance of resisting 'the pull towards' standardization and instrumentalism" (Burnard, 2006). Historical examples (i.e., the 1999-2000 UNAM student occupation) reveal that academic marketization is not universally supported and can be resisted. Scholars are encouraged to remember that they possess the access, resources and theoretical background necessary to challenge the "taken-for-granted notions of managerial discourse." Such resources could serve the purpose of preserving the original goal of the university – to allow for understanding of the world and "the development of human potential" (Clegg, 2008). The educational curriculum at university settings should encourage inquiry, sovereign thought and "confidence to argue from alternative viewpoints" (Hargreaves, 2008).

Discussion

Similarly to "emotional experiences...described as socially constructed...ways of being" (*Emotions, 1.7*), social "pressures" are thought to have shaped the neuro-functional properties of the human brain. Hence, the collective programming or conditioning of the human brain and emotional experiences to suit a corporate profit-driven educational discourse is not only feasible, but also grounded in reality (i.e., U.S. mainstream education seeking to "overcome cultural diversity and personal uniqueness" and "discipline the developing energies of young people" as a means through which "to mold a loyal citizenry and an effective workforce for the growing industrial system"). Such finding may help explain the prevention of positive emotions derived through evidence-based practices within educational settings. Since spirituality-inspired positive affect leads to expanded consciousness, students have the potential to sense that the knowledge they are imparted in mainstream academic settings is in juxtaposition to what they are innately motivated to learn. Refusing to participate in public educational discourse and creating a reality different from the one manufactured for them to experience inevitably leads to the collapse of the corporate profit-based educational agenda.

2.2 Pedagogy

"There is resistance to creating new citizens with new minds…Most of what we offer children in school is ill designed (McDermott, 1992). The rise of "one best way" to pedagogy possibly limits the "creative space within which teachers exercise professional judgment" (Burnard & White, 2008). The teacher loses the opportunity to create a "living experience" for students when he or she teaches in accordance to a strictly adhered to "pre-packaged lesson plan" (Nicholson, 2000).

***

The focus of traditional educational systems is primarily on the analytical ability, fostering critical, yet not creative thought (Loia & Dillon, 2006), "seeking knowledge, rather than seeking meaning" (Goral, 2010). "In the USA today, education is brain-oriented; goals are cognitive, intellectual, and academic. We focus on the head, not the hands and heart" (Sobo, 2012). Krishnamurti also noticed the tendency of education, particularly Western education, to stress entirely on nurturing the intellect or the brain while failing to foster the development of the body, spirit and soul (Miller, 1999). "Meaning is no longer found through the soul by dwelling in the world with reverence, but imposed by the calculating mind, which assigns everything a value or a utilitarian purpose" (Miller, 2001).

34

Steiner did not oppose dualism, "per se," yet he perceived a problem with dualism that "pays attention only to the *separation*. While human beings have to separate phenomenon to understand it, "in reality...life is 'a unity' and 'a living whole.'" Real understanding, therefore, "does not still things," but rather attributes meaning to them (Sobo, 2012). Krishnamurti (1953) adds that fragmentation is "a central problem in modern life." Life in present times has been divided into such a great number of departments that the only meaning of education is that it allows for learning a specific skill or profession. Rather than "awakening the integrated intelligence" of a person, education encourages an individual to "conform to a pattern" thus preventing "his comprehension of himself as a total process." Seeking to solve the numerous existential problems at their respective categorical levels "indicates an utter lack of comprehension" (Miller, 1999). Eckersley reflected on the "contemporary crises of youth" as "a profound and growing failure of western culture...to provide a sense of meaning, belonging, and purpose in our lives, as well as a framework of values" (Gidley, 2010). Anna Craft (The Open University, UK) concurs by stating that education lacks "reference to values" (Burnard, 2006).

***

Young children adapt rapidly to expectations (Geist & Hohn, 2009). "Early learning contexts require children to sit still, attend, follow directions, and approach/enter group play - all very challenging accomplishments" (Denham et al., 2012)! "Diligently engaging on a tedious assignment despite an overwhelming desire to do something more pleasant is" a "difficult task for most students" (Galla et al., 2014). School becomes a dreary place for children if they are instructed to sit silently and engage in projects lacking daily-life contextual meaning, requiring memorization, following rules and recitation instead of divergent thinking and creative abilities (Geist & Hohn, 2009). Students feel bored when the material being taught is of low value to them, when they are given little to no choice over the learning activity, when the learning task is more challenging compared to their skill level and when their skills exceed the complexity of the task. Students feel confusion when the material being taught is difficult to understand, when they are not sure as to how to proceed with a particular learning task and when they "encounter challenging impasses." Students feel frustrated when they make repeated mistakes, when they are unable to move forward or when significant goals are being blocked. Lastly, students feel a sense of desperation and anxiety when "their efforts seem futile" and when failure results in negative outcomes.

On the contrary, students feel curious and interested when they indulge in topics of interest to them and when they encounter new learning material. They feel "*eureka moments*" when insights are gained and significant discoveries are made. Students feel delighted when obstacles are overcome and goals are met. Lastly, students experience a sense of engagement when the learning goals are clear, there is a balance between the difficulty of the learning task and the skills required to solve it and when immediate feedback is provided on partaken actions (D'Mello, 2013). Klein (1990, p. 27) adds that "most learning takes place when young children are actively engaged in...experimenting, experiencing, and raising their own questions and finding answers" (Zachopouloua et al., 2006). Provided that every person's brain is "uniquely organized" and since too little or too much of a particular chemical (i.e., dopamine) affects a child's mood and their willingness to learn, "it takes a special educator to not want to force each child into a lockstep curriculum" (Rushton, 2011).

2.3 Performance, Standardization, Monitoring

"The educational climate during the past decade has been affected by ever tighter state and federal control over learning, leading to still further testing, politically mandated outcomes and national standards" (Miller). According to Hartley (2006), the educational system is "decidedly performance-driven, standardized and monitored" (Burnard & White, 2008).

2.3.1 Performance

Performance is an essential component of global educational reform today. Lyotard (1984) defines performativity in systems as the predisposition to value effectiveness and efficiency as a means to achieving the "greatest 'output'...Assessed teacher performance" as "the direct focus of change...has substantially impacted the work of teachers." Being a teacher today incorporates "expectations of compliance and performance" and ignorance of teachers' "beliefs, theories, epistemologies, practices and agency." Benchmarks and standards as measurements of achievement do not always represent the values of teachers, in particular, and schools at large. The state commands "what is to be taught, when it is to be taught, and increasingly, how is it to be taught." Teachers' failure of "performativity" could result in adverse consequences, including "non-renewal of contracts and emotional exhaustion, chronic stress and teacher burnout" (Burnard & White, 2008).

2.3.2 Standardization

Teachers are mandated to test and measure students and "to report using mandated standards and systems" (Burnard & White, 2008). "The increasing standardization of learning prepares young people to act aggressively, cleverly, and resourcefully in the job market and the competitive corporate world. It contributes little or nothing to decent communities, loving relationships, or ways to transcend self-centeredness" (Miller, 2001). It is therefore critical that "we extract ourselves from the current paradigm and move from 'miseducation to mindful education'" (Goral, 2010). "Humans are multi-dimensional and transcendental beings." According to Victor Frankl, "humans find fulfillment only when their needs for meaning and purpose are adequately met" (Vayalilkarottu, 2012).

2.3.3 Monitoring

School performance monitoring has been a topic of "intense interest in most parts of the world." The International Institute for Educational Planning (IIEP), for instance, "has a large school supervision project" dedicated to the topic of school performance monitoring. The IIEP designates school supervision as "the control and support of schools and teachers, the promotion of change, and interchange of information between schools and administration centres." School supervisors are viewed as inspectors of teachers who are "often poorly resourced, and with too many responsibilities."

A number of countries are still relying on external inspection as the primary tool for school supervision, yet an increasing number of countries are implementing school self-review as the primary supervisory tool or a combination of school self-review and external school inspection. "In practice, this often means that the employment of principals and teachers (and system administrators) is conditional upon improving performance on system wide tests of student learning" (Gurr).

2.4 Teacher Accountability

Accountability consists of three components: moral, conceptual and professional. Moral accountability is focused on "meeting the needs of parents and students," conceptual – on "meeting the requirements of the system" and professional – on "meeting one's own expectations and those of colleagues" (Gurr).

Discussion

Deliberately compromised spirituality appears to be the driving force of the ultimate goal of education – corporate profit. Sovereignty and expansion of consciousness are obstructed and strictly confined within the scope of the educational agenda when: a) teachers' "beliefs, theories, epistemologies, practices and agency" are ignored; b) through "standardization of learning," students are being prepared "to act aggressively, cleverly, and resourcefully in the job market and the competitive corporate world," contributing "little or nothing to decent communities, loving relationships, or ways to transcend self-centeredness." Teacher accountability, noncompliance and "school self-review" measures further ensure that educational personnel will personify, implement and achieve the corporate-serving goal of mainstream education.

2.5 Creativity Re-Defined

The focus on creativity today is being transformed from "'create' as a verb to 'creativity' as a noun" (Craft & Jeffrey, 2008).

***

"The paradox is omnipresent. All around us, more and more aspects of life are being standardized, prefabricated, and defined. On the other hand, human social development is unthinkable without imagination and creativity...A wealth of ideas, mental/spiritual flexibility, and imagination are required of adults...to enable them to shape their lives" (Lang, 2003). "A disjuncture is identified between the commodification of education arising from managerialism and consumerism and the spirit and energy that constitutes the creative impulse" (Clegg, 2008).

As a result of the No Child Left Behind Act (NCLB), the effectiveness of school administrators is exponentially being evaluated on the basis of students' achievement on standardized tests resulting in "widespread reduction in subjects not addressed" by the Act (Humphries et al., 2011). Schools have removed the tools necessary to promote creativity while more attention has been given to reading and math instead.

Overpowering assessment and testing requirements, time constraints, academic priorities, educational directives on local school and federal level as well as lack of capital for creativity-based activities had translated into the eradication of arts in schools. The decline of arts (i.e., art; music) and physical education in schools began prior to the enactment of NCLB. However, NCLB increased their rate of decline (Geist & Hohn, 2009). 71% of 15,000 U.S. school districts increased learning time for reading and math at the expense of other subjects, such as music and history instruction. A different study reported a 22% decrease in music and art instructional time on an elementary-school level as a direct result of NCLB test requirements (Persellin, 2007). Standardized testing in public U.S. schools is designed to correct for the "relatively poor learning outcomes." Yet, the reduced physical activity resulting from greater focus on standardized assessment has contributed to "lower academic achievement rates" (Sobo, 2012). "It is important that classroom teachers, as well as physical education and music teachers, find ways to meet students' needs and interests

and maximize musical and physical education experiences"
(Humphries et al., 2011).

***

Economic globalization has contributed to the
"universalizing" and "politisation" of creativity (Burnard &
White, 2008). Since the late 1990s, policy makers in a
number of regions of the world (i.e., Japan; Hong Kong;
Scotland; Singapore; Australia; the United States; Canada)
have increasingly called for creativity in education within the
context of economic development (Craft, 2006). Influenced
by "business leaders," governments aim at introducing "new
kinds of...creative capital." Creativity must be developed in
the early educational years "in order for companies to reap
ideas and innovation...Creativity 'inputs' for children at
primary school will result in creative 'outputs' by these
children when they become adult workers" (Burnard &
White, 2008). Evidence of creativity policy is embedded
within "the support and development of what the
Government refers to as the creative industries" (i.e., music;
information and communications technology; film). The
Creative Britain document is a most recent exemplification of
the centralization of "creativity policy made by the
Government." "Creativity is now a value in itself...and there
is more pressure not only to be creative but to audit it."
(Craft & Jeffrey, 2008). Hartley (2006) proposes that the
time when creativity in schools will be formally "managed
and monitored...as sets of competences and outcomes is not
as far as it might first appear (Burnard & White, 2008).
        "The call for creativity in education," based on a
"market-driven foundation," is, however, characterized by
"fundamental problems." The first problem is that universal
or centralized creativity excludes "macro- or subcultural
values." The second problem is that "the drive to
innovate...becomes an end in itself" when embedded within

41

the context of making profit. Products and services replaced by new ones become obsolete and are disposed of instead of being restored or repaired (Craft, 2006).

Discussion

Academic achievement seems to serve two basic functions. First, it is a distraction or a disguise to the actual objective of dissolving spirituality for it is a dichotomy to enact a law, the very name of which expresses a determination to not leave a child struggling with academic performance behind and yet, simultaneously, remove the very subjects which ensure academic success (i.e., "reduced physical activity" resulting in "lower academic achievement rates;" removal of arts programs). Second, academic achievement becomes in and of itself the means through which spirituality is compromised when learning is strictly confined within corporate-driven mainstream curriculum outlines.

Furthermore, research findings demonstrated that the removal of evidence and spirituality-based subjects such as physical education and arts from educational discourse "began prior to the enactment of NCLB" and was followed by an exponential increase. Aware of the free will to choose and create one's reality, it is likely that the informal enactment of the law served the function of an experimental phase designed to assess the degree of opposition towards the intended legal change. Little or no resistance could have been perceived as an indication that the law would not be disapproved of to a point of threatening the continual unfoldment of the corporate-serving educational agenda. Alternatively, and/or parallel to the latter inference, the informal stage of NCLB could have been intended as a desensitization phase. Such and similar implications raise the questions of how far in the past did the corporate profit-driven educational agenda begin to unfold and where is it pre-contemplated to ultimately lead.

2.6 Sorting

In a socially segregated system, "disadvantaged pupils face the double disadvantage of a negative school-composition effect as well as the influence of their own disadvantaged background." Research has shown that, on average, secondary school systems with socially segregated schools perform more poorly in reading and math (Croxford & David Raffe, 2013).

***

The American society is increasingly being divided between people with financial stability, educational credentials and employment and those without. Unequal opportunity is at the core of the cultural problem of American public education. "The public schools, despite the efforts of millions of concerned teachers and administrators, have in fact fallen deeply into the job of sorting out those who will have access to the rewards of our culture from those who will not." In other words, "despite our claimed commitments to equal opportunity in education, our schools are well organized to sort out children by the most arbitrary criteria into two normal piles, namely, those who succeed and those who fail...In a system in which everyone is measured against everyone else, the only way of doing well is to do better than someone else. Every success makes a failure, and every failure makes a success. For every child who makes an advance in New York City, a child in Detroit is pushed down a notch" (McDermott, 1992).

Furthermore, the American educational system "has increasingly become the national institution that most efficiently levels aspirations and sorts each new generation into approximately the same configuration as the previous generation." Qualitative research findings revealed that parents of high socio-economic status had greater opportunity to choose a specific school for their children compared to parents of lower socio-economic status. Higher social-class parents tended to choose schools that were, on average, higher on the socio-economic ladder and exceeded academically (Croxford & David Raffe, 2013).

Last, but not least, "school systems need to rethink how they manage schooling...Not all students should be expected to want or need a college preparatory track, but many schools have no real alternative for the students to value. The explicit message in many schools is that the college preparation track is the valued track, and the other tracks are for students who cannot manage the work. Vocational, agricultural, and technological education should be a viable alternative for these students, but schools often fail to offer high quality programs in these areas, or, when present, these programs might be viewed as dumping grounds for disenfranchised or hopeless students rather than challenging programs with real value" (Osborne, 2004).

Discussion

A question was raised in section *1.4.2 (Music)* regarding the implementation of music education programs solely in more affluent schools. Results from the qualitative study suggested that "parents of high socio-economic status had greater opportunity to choose a specific school for their children compared to parents of lower socio-economic status. Higher social-class parents tended to choose schools that were, on average, higher on the socio-economic ladder and exceeded academically." At the same time, United States education "has increasingly become the national institution that most efficiently levels aspirations and sorts each new generation into approximately the same configuration as the previous generation." A reason why parents of higher socio-economic status are allocated the opportunity to choose a more affluent school for their children may hence be embedded in the fact that such parents are active participants in the corporate-profit agenda (i.e., "have access to the rewards of our culture") and more prone to influence their children in the same direction. Children of such parents who choose to pursue a career in music are therefore more likely to comply with the expectations of the agenda and ensure the generation of profit for the "creative industries" (*Creativity Re-Defined, 2.5*).

2.7 Special Education and Inclusive Education

An increasing number of students are being placed in special needs education programs (Kiviuori & Salmi, 2009). It has been established that students' sense of belonging at educational settings is compromised by peer rejection and isolation. Inclusive education, "currently high on the (political) agendas of many countries," aims at educating all students, including students with special educational needs (SEN), in the general education classroom (Pijl et al., 2008).

Discussion

Research findings demonstrated that, "challenged by meeting deadlines, course outcomes and examination board requirements...highly creative children had the lowest chance of academic success" (*Education, 1.3.2.3*). In an attempt to generalize to the wider student body, those who are not inclined to "learning a specific skill or profession" (*Pedagogy, 2.2*), as outlined by educational expectations, require the special need for re-education, re-programming or re-conditioning into compliance with corporate goals.

2.8 Development

Contrary to empirical findings, conventional child development theories "presume" that human behavior is linear; "that development follows continuous straight or curved trajectories." Any deviation from the linear expectation of developmental trajectory is perceived to "reflect random fluctuations or measurement errors." Secondly, traditional theories assume that "all aspects of the final developmental outcome are laid down in pre-existing structures, specifically, in the genes and/or the environment." Similarly, current child developmental theories propose that "all structures that the mind can create must be present before that creation occurs." Such theory precludes the possibility of novel data presenting itself during development. Thelen & Smith (1998, p. 564) object to such theories by asking: "If the instructions to develop are in the genes, who turns on the genes? If the complexity exists in the environment, who decides what the organism should absorb and retain?" There is a great diversity of developmental trajectories and novel ways to solve developmental challenges.

Lastly, established child development theories fail to incorporate the array of developmental domains (i.e., cognitive and emotional development) in explaining child development and limit their scope to specific developmental domains instead (Cupit, 2007). The Bronfenbrenner (1979) ecological systems theory postulates that "child development is diverse, complex" and influenced by the interaction between the child and his or her environment (Rafferty, 2013).

Discussion

"Contrary to empirical findings," the theory of linear and predictable development appears to lay the foundation for the global standardization of learning. Absolute control over development or learning translates into absolute power over spirituality and full compliance with the educational agenda. By ensuring the prevention of "novel data" entering the human experience through means such as learning-related monitoring, reporting, supervision, accountability and negative consequences related to noncompliance, mainstream education is manufacturing a new paradigm of human development - one which, if allowed to continue unfolding, could eventually become fully predictable and supported by empirical findings.

2.9 Cognitive Intelligence

A "pernicious idea" in existence, suggests that astute people are fast all the time and that slowness is the equivalent of stupidity (Claxton, 2006).

***

The debate as to whether intelligence is a singular attribute or a "plethora of components" has predominated the 20th century (Gardner & Moran, 2006). The goal of early research into cognition was to "objectively describe cognitive development and to scientifically define intelligence through establishing predictable empirical stages of advancement. The notion of Intelligence Quotient (IQ) became the scientific benchmark to profile a learner's intellectual capacities and educational possibilities."

Cognitive scientists with Howard Gardner "at the forefront" objected to the "notion of a universal IQ standardization" as intelligence could not be measured in definite terms under scientific conditions (Chaudhary & Aswal, 2013). The brain is in a constant state of flux – "continually growing, changing and adapting to the environment." Hence, intelligence is not a "fixed" phenomenon, but rather fluctuating as a direct result of environmental stimuli, hormonal fluctuations and chemical reactions. Biological and environmental stimuli lead to more than 100 billion of neurological connections formed within the cerebral cortex during the first 5 years of life. Neurons are being overproduced during the early years of life so that "the child can be supported to navigate through life." Learning a language or making decisions as to when to walk, talk, crawl are neuron-dependent activities that contribute to the establishment of strong neuronal connections. Recalling information occurs more robustly and rapidly when the connections between neurons are strong. If not used, a large number of formed neurons die out. "Early childhood educators literally have the ability to help shape a child's mind" (Rushton, 2011).

In 1983, relying on "empirical findings of hundreds of studies from a variety of disciplines" (i.e., cognitive science; anthropology; evolutionary sciences; neuroscience) as opposed to psychometric and experimental psychological findings alone as was "the dominant approach to intelligence at the time," Gardner established the theory of multiple intelligences (MI). According to Garner's MI theory, there are eight or more types of intelligence (Humphries et al., 2011). Gardner did not claim that MI theory embodied the "definite description of human cognitive capacities." Gardner attested that human cognition is more comprehensively understood when somewhat independent, yet interacting intelligences are taken into consideration "than do competing accounts" (Gardner & Moran, 2006). "Teaching to only one or two kinds of intelligence, such as linguistic and logical-mathematical, is common but does not take advantage of students' potential" (Humphries et al., 2011).

Children's perception about the nature of intelligence could have an impact on their learning. In comparison to children who perceive intelligence on a developmental trajectory spectrum, there is a greater likelihood that children would "disengage" from a learning task if they believe that intelligence is fixed and their performance on a learning task is negatively evaluated (Miele et al., 2013). Based on 2007 estimates, 200 million children under the age of 5 in less developed countries do not reach their cognitive development potential during their childhood and adolescent years (Camargo-Figuera et al., 2014).

Discussion

The research finding that, if not used, a great number of formed neurons "die out," lends additional support to the means through which conditioning to the corporate-educational agenda takes place. Mandated standardized learning automatically translates into the exclusion of learning possibilities outside the scope of formal academic material. Corporate-shaped mainstream educational content therefore becomes the border within which learning takes place.

2.10 Emotional Intelligence

Emotional intelligence (EI) was introduced as a construct by Salovey and Mayer in 1990 and expanded upon by Goleman (1998). According to Goleman, emotional intelligence consists of 4 domains - self and social awareness, self and relationship management, each comprised of a number of subskills. "The central claim was that every person is a leader in some manner, and every leader's main obligation is to create resonance, that is, to "'prime good feelings in those they lead' which in turn will generate the best behavior in others." EI theory has "been recommended for improving classroom learning...applied in classroom activities" and has had "widespread circulation in education."

　　Yet, EI theory "lacks a unitary empirically supported construct" and is "not consistent with relevant cognitive neuroscience findings." Given the lack of scientific support, the "continuing acceptance" of EI theory in education "might...be considered educational malpractice." Teaching EI theory harms teachers, students and the field of education at large. While teachers are being taught an "insufficiently supported" theory "of human cognition," students are unlikely to benefit from EI as the theory lacks "sound empirical support." The field of education is harmed as EI contradicts with the "core values of education," namely "the discovery of valid ideas supported by a preponderance of sound evidence." The National Research Council (2000) has established a standard which states that high school students "should learn that a scientific theory... 'must abide by the rules of evidence.'" When used "as the basis for education practices," theories such as EI "are replacing other classroom practices that may be of greater benefit for students." It is concluded that "if the search for truth is discarded from the purposes of human learning, then...the integrity of learning...is lost." Until theories such as EI "have garnered reasonable evidentiary support they should not be applied in education" (Waterhouse, 2006a).

Discussion

The duplicitous practices of mainstream education are exemplified by the fact that academic approaches radically contradict with a prime educational value of evidence-based "discovery" while it is the expectation of mainstream education that students "abide by the rules of evidence." Stated otherwise, rules of evidence apply only to oppressed human beings, not to the orchestrators of oppression.

It is moreover contradictory that the educational agenda seeks to prevent the experience of positive emotions (i.e., removal of arts programs), yet propagates the theory of Emotional Intelligence, designed to "create resonance" or "prime good feelings" in human beings led by a leader. The reason for and the means through which public education seeks to achieve such objective is a point of inquiry.

2.11 Spiritual Intelligence

"Spiritual Intelligence is a term used to indicate spiritual correlate to IQ and EQ (Emotional Quotient)." Author Stephen Covey defines Spiritual Intelligence (SI) as "the central and most fundamental of all the intelligences, because it becomes the source of guidance for the other[s]." Howard Gardner's termed SI "existential intelligence." According to David B. King, SI is comprised of 4 main "abilities of capacities:" critical existence thinking (i.e., the capacity to critically examine the nature of reality, existence, space, time and other metaphysical and existential matters), personal meaning production (i.e., the ability to interpret and find purpose from mental and physical experiences), transcendental awareness (i.e., the capacity to "identify transcendent dimensions/patterns of the self, of others and of physical world") and conscious state expansion (i.e., the ability to access and exit higher states of consciousness at will such as through meditation). SI is realizing one self and living a self-realized life. It is comprised of "skills and abilities that empower you to live in harmony with your highest values and move unswervingly towards your life goals" (Chaudhary & Aswal, 2013).

"The United Nations *Convention on the Rights of the Child* (2004) includes spirituality as an aspect of life that should be developed through education" (Mountain, 2007). Despite the advocacy of a number of educational researchers worldwide to incorporate spirituality in education, "very little 'evolution of consciousness' literature appears in educational discourses" while "the imperative to educate children with the evolution of consciousness in mind has been largely overlooked in mainstream education" (Gidley, 2007). "Spiritual development has been given lip service in much of the educational literature" (Mountain, 2007). While almost all topics are comfortably discussed in education, "religion and spirituality are taboo in the halls of education, unless they are analyzed in a strictly detached way" (Corrigan, 2010). The spiritual problem of American public education is embedded in the fact that "questions about the meaning of life are asked to stay in the shadows." The academic curriculum focuses on "mastery before mystery, fact before fantasy, and winning before wonder" (McDermott, 1992). According to Rudolf Steiner, wonder is a critical precursor to thinking. In his own words: "It is absolutely essential that before we begin to think, before we so much as begin to set our thinking in motion, we experience the condition of wonder" (Almon).

Advocates of integrating spirituality in education "call for an opening of the heart so that we may once again instill meaning, wonder, and awe into the education of our children. They suggest valuing community over competition, caring and compassion within academics, and an infusion of the arts into the curriculum" (Goral, 2010). A SI curriculum may include instruction as well as practices (i.e., meditation; mindfulness; spiritual guidance; studying spiritual text). "The new role of the teacher is to become a moral philosopher" (Chaudhary & Aswal, 2013).

Discussion

From actively preventing the experience of spirituality-based positive emotions, equality and the creation of "new citizens with new minds" (*Pedagogy, 2.2*) to standardizing learning and ignoring "the imperative to educate children with the evolution of consciousness in mind," the pattern of mainstream education resisting the implementation of spirituality-based best practices in education continues to solidify. It is not coincidental that the topic of spirituality "has been given lip service in much of the educational literature" while "questions about the meaning of life are asked to stay in the shadows." To reiterate, spirituality extends beyond the artificial borders of existence raised by mainstream education and opens doors to alternative creative avenues, which may not serve the corporate profit-based goal of the educational agenda.

2.12 Recess

"There is an alarming trend, especially in the United States, toward the reduction of recess during the school day" which "directly contravenes the *Convention on the Rights of the Child*" addressing "rest and relaxation" (Moore, 1997). There are recommendations to confine movement in public schools to "activity breaks" (Sobo, 2012).

Discussion

Physical activity is directly associated with improved physical and psychological health (*Physical Activity, 1.10*). Recess, in particular, is synonymous to "rest and relaxation" or the experience of spirituality-based positive emotion. Hence, the removal of recess automatically translates into lesser than optimal physical, psychological and emotional health. Compromised well-being subsequently leads to limited awareness or choices confined within the scope of the educational agenda.

2.13 Nature and Outdoor Access

"Children are experiential beings." Bronfenbrenner's theory postulates that children experience reality through their senses. "Sensory experiences link the child's exterior world with their interior, hidden, affective world." The stimulus for personal development is derived from within an individual as a reflection of his or her specific needs "at any point in time." Such needs are so diverse and complex that "there is no possible way they can be matched by environments managed as resources based on predictive needs, as 'bureaucracies' often do." Such an approach is only suitable "to resolve very specific developmental problems."

"A growing number of professionals are beginning to express concern that children are spending less time outdoors." Historically, creating open areas for children "has never been the top priority for city planning." Informally used by children outdoor city areas such as waterfronts, have been recently either re-constructed or fenced "as urban land use has become much more tightly planned or *re*planned...Children are losing access to outdoor space." Television, computers and electronic games are contributing to children's prolonged stay indoors, especially when "the outdoors is insufficiently diverse and attractive to 'pull' them out to play and explore."

***

"Most alarming is the fact that children are losing contact with nature in their daily lives." Nature is the optimal option for children to choose stimulants as "it offers constantly changing diversity and the broadest range of possible interactions...Nature is capable of stimulating "children's development in ways not provided by other means... The natural environment offers the diversity of experience that children seek." Since the natural environment is the principal source of sensory stimulation, freedom to explore and play with the outdoor environment through the senses in their own space and time is vital for healthy development of an interior life. "Daily hands-on contact with natural settings is essential to children's health...Informal play provides us with primary experience of nature, through which our values are formed...Because of their constantly changing diversity, natural settings provide a richer spectrum of choice for supporting prosocial behavior among children...A rich, open environment will continuously present alternative choices for creative engagement. A rigid, bland environment will limit healthy growth and development of the individual...a boring environment will likely lead to antisocial, unhealthy behavior."

Study findings reveal that the presence of nature is the primary reason for children's positive feelings towards their school environment. It has been demonstrated that natural school settings contribute to increased students' attention span, longer periods of time spent in group activity, greater levels of positive social interaction, "far more mixing by age, sex, and ethnic background" and an overall "more creative and peaceful" atmosphere compared to a synthetic (i.e., asphalt) school environment. Natural school settings had been further found to "stimulate all aspects and stages of child development through multi-sensory experience" (i.e., cognitive development; creativity; imagination; enhanced self-esteem; greater understanding of natural principles). "School buildings surrounded by asphalt, chain-link fencing, and prohibitive notices communicate control, authority, and unfriendliness" (Moore, 1997).

Discussion

Economic growth takes precedence over children's well-being when the priority for city planning is not children's healthy development while open spaces informally used by children are being fenced or re-constructed.

Additionally, informal interaction with nature contributes to healthy development. Thus, as the inner self is capable and inclined to shape the external world into resonance with the state within (*Emotions, 1.7*), so is the external environment capable of influencing and achieving resonance with internal experiences of reality. Limiting the opportunities to interact with natural settings prevents developmental choice and expansion, confining children to well-defined outlines of a synthetic educational environment with which to interact. Such artificially-created surrounding hence has the potential to shape students' values into resonance with the principles of the academic system, namely self-serving profit achieved through power over others. Personification of educational values ensures the continual unfoldment of the corporate-driven educational agenda.

2.14 Uncomfortable Thoughts & Emotions

"Unwanted, intrusive thoughts, images, and impulses are reported by 80% to 90% of the general population. Unwanted, intrusive thoughts are normally evoked by external stimuli, stressful situations and negative emotional states" (Fairbrother et al., 2014). Instead of allowing young people the space required to process uncomfortable emotions, society tends to label and diagnose such experiences as a disease. Young people's distress is numbed with prescription medications, which leads to dis-attachment from one's true self and prevention of growth (Jureidini, 2014).

Discussion

Imagination is associated with cognition and emotions (*Personal Identity, 1.3.1.1*) and with spirituality at large (*Education, 1.2.2*). Spiritual Intelligence (SI) is correlated with Intelligence Quotient (IQ) and Emotional Quotient (EQ) (*Spiritual Intelligence, 2.11*). All SI, IQ and EQ are associated with the environment (*Nature and Outdoor Access, 2.13*). The removal of spirituality-based opportunities from educational curriculums thus automatically translates into the difficulty of engaging the imagination to perceive alternatives to the negative emotion-evoking educational possibilities. The finding that "80% to 90% of the general population" experiences negative psychological states is hence logical and a clear demonstration of the validity of the profit-based educational agenda, deliberately unfolding through the dissolution of spirituality. Such high prevalence is a robust indication of its statistically significant success.

Furthermore, mainstream education does not seem to be the sole orchestrator of the corporate-profit agenda. Mental health services appear to apply approaches alike the ones implemented by the educational system. Similarly to previous findings regarding the effects resulting from the suppression of speech (*Language Development, 1.11*) and emotions (*Emotions, 1.7*), it is herein stated that young people dis-attach from their "true self" while their personal growth is compromised when they are diagnosed and "numbed with prescription medications" instead of being allowed the space to process "uncomfortable emotions." Hence, in striking resemblance to educational practices, the unfoldment of spiritual development is blocked.

2.15 Anxiety

"Anxiety disorders are among the most prevalent psychiatric conditions in children and adolescents and, in the United States, may affect 15–20% of youth" (Strawn et al., 2014). Between 7.4% and 17.3% of 4-year old children experience subclinical levels of anxiety (Buss, 2011). In most general terms, anxiety contributes to feelings of apprehension, fear, worry, nervousness and hypertension (Zhang et al., 2011). Poverty, trauma, maltreatment and parental psychopathology are some of the identified environmental factors leading to anxiety (Buss, 2011).

Discussion

One of the leading causes of anxiety amongst children and adolescents is maltreatment. Therefore, through inequality, mandating standardized learning, removing opportunities for spirituality-based positive experiences (i.e., resisting best practices in education), implementing approaches contradicting research findings and teachers projecting anxiety onto students (i.e., anxiety was "found to be the most prevalent emotion experienced by teachers," *Emotions, 1.7*), the educational system is directly responsible for the alarming prevalence of anxiety disorders amongst youth. By labeling and numbing young adults who experience uncomfortable emotions with prescription medications, leading to "dis-attachment from one's true self and prevention of growth" (*Uncomfortable Thoughts and Emotions, 2.14*) (i.e., maltreatment), mental health services are also accountable for childhood and adolescence anxiety disorders.

Last, but not least, suppression of speech (*Language Development, 1.11*) and emotions (*Emotions, 1.7*) projected by parents onto their children as they had been projected onto them during their educational experience could be viewed as "parental psychopathology" or a different way the educational system is straightforwardly causing epidemic rates of anxiety amongst youth.

2.15.1 Test Anxiety

Children and adolescents are subject to repeated tests and examinations designed to evaluate their academic achievement level and further academic potential. "Passing or failing the examinations mostly has strong consequences for future development. As challenging situations, these examinations provide a certain amount of stress for most persons" (Spangler, 1997). In fact, "academic examinations and school work are considered to be the most stressful events of adolescent's life" (Mary et al., 2014). Stressful situations activate the sympathetic nervous system and the hypothalamic-pituitary-adrenocrotical (HPA) axis, leading to the release of stress hormones (i.e., cortisol;

catecholamines). "Stress hormones may lead to the dysregulation of bodily functions, including the immune, cardiovascular and metabolic functions" (Cohen & Khalaila, 2014). Emotional responses such as anxiety can also be observed as a result of stressful situations (Spangler, 1997). 179 university students were divided into two groups – exam-stress and control group. Emotional well-being and perceived stress were assessed at two time points – at baseline and during a 2-week exam session. Findings revealed that the exam-stress group experienced significantly greater levels of perceived stress and a decline in emotional well-being during the exam session compared to baseline (Pollard et al., 1995).

Between 25% and 30% of students experience test anxiety (Orbach et al., 2007). Test anxiety generally involves a feeling of worry in evaluation-based situations (Wachelka & Katz, 1999). Students may be subjected to experiencing anxiety at varying degree during an exam (Zhang et al., 2011). Test anxiety is disproportionately distributed amongst minority students and students with learning disabilities (Wachelka & Katz, 1999). "The excessive worry and intrusive thoughts about performance that students with test anxiety experience are predictors of emotional and psychological distress." From all psychological disorders, test anxiety aligns to social phobia to a most pronounced degree as it can cause an individual to "experience fear of entering into social situations due to concerns about poor performance and embarrassment" (Rajiah & Saravanan, 2014). "High test anxiety is…associated with low self esteem…disruptive classroom behavior" and "negative attitudes toward school" (Wachelka & Katz, 1999).

Test anxiety can also exert an adverse effect on students' motivation and academic performance. Studies found that test anxiety is associated with both low extrinsic motivation and amotivation and is one of the main factors leading to low academic performance (Rajiah & Saravanan,

2014). "High test anxiety is...associated with poor reading and math achievement" and "failing grades" (Wachelka & Katz, 1999). Math and reading skills are prerequisites for academic success, "social and economic opportunities." Recently, 40% of fourth-grade United States students have failed to achieve basic level of reading proficiency, 25% of fifth-grade students were not able to solve math problems involving fractions and less than 50% of fifth-grade students were able to solve math word problems involving rate and measurement (Valiente et al., 2014).

Lastly, severe anxiety can lead to negative consequences in life (Zhang et al., 2011) as 20% of students experiencing test anxiety withdraw from school prior to graduation as a result of "repeated academic failure" (Wachelka & Katz, 1999). Students who fail to graduate with a high school diploma are subject to health, substance abuse and interpersonal problems to a greater extent compared to students who complete high school. They are also not as likely to be employed or to earn as much as graduates do (Lynch et al., 2014).

Discussion

The high prevalence of text anxiety and the low academic achievement associated with it provide further evidence that academic achievement is not the means through which the educational agenda seeks to achieve the goal of corporate profit. Otherwise, "academic examinations and school work," leading to test anxiety and school drop-out, would be removed and replaced by best practices in education (i.e., arts-integrated curriculum). Rather, mainstream education is achieving the goal of corporate profit through the reiterated herein dissolution of spirituality as exemplified by students' compromised quality of health, motivation, psychological state and life, directly resulting from detrimental mainstream educational practices.

2.15.1.1 Fear Appeals

Fear appeal is a terms used to describe "persuasive messages designed to facilitate a course of action so as to avoid a negative outcome." Fear appeals originated in the health sector and generalized to educational settings. Fear appeals in academic settings are delivered prior to test administration or examination, are focused on the adverse outcomes of failure and are thus designed to evoke fear in students. According to Putwain and Symes (2011a, 2011b), test anxiety is "related to the degree to which messages are perceived as *threatening*." Study findings revealed that "students...report lower self-determined motivation" and lower scores on a math exam when the fear appeals directed by teachers are more frequent and "perceived as threatening." Results further demonstrated that students scored higher on a math exam when the fear appeals were less frequently used and perceived as less threatening (Putwain & Remedios, 2014).

Discussion

In line with previous findings (i.e. academic achievement; equality), educators and the public are being deceived that the purpose of fear appeals, in particular, is to "facilitate a course of action as to avoid a negative outcome" when research findings clearly demonstrate that fear appeals lead to the exact opposite of the stated outcome – lower, not higher, academic achievement.

Furthermore, in addition to the governmental sectors of mainstream education and mental health, through implementing contradictory to best practices methods (namely fear appeals), the health care sector also appears to be a participant in the corporate-profit agenda and its methods.

2.16 Noncompliance

Noncompliance has been defined as "not following a direction within a reasonable amount of time...Child noncompliance is...one of the most frequently reported problems by parents and teachers" and is a possible precursor to "more serious disruptive and delinquent behaviors later in adolescents" (Bellipanni et al., 2013). Behaviors such as yelling, whining, ignoring requests and complaining comprise the response class of noncompliance (Carrington & Kratochwill, 1994). Noncompliant behavior could significantly impede children's academic success and negatively affect students' personal and social well-being (Lee, 2005).

Noncompliance may serve three particular behavioral functions within the classroom setting: mild escape or avoidance, extreme aversion, and attention seeking. Often times, non-compliant behavior serves a mild escape or avoidance function when teachers assign tasks that are perceived as aversive to the student and when no tangible rewards are provided upon completion of the task. In such instances, reducing the engagement time with the task through noncompliant behavior such as ignoring the teacher's request, getting out of seat, engaging in more enjoyable activity or verbally refusing to complete the task serves as the motivating factor for the maintenance of the noncompliant behavior. In brief, the student learns that the more his or her noncompliance serves the function of decreasing his or her engagement time with the aversive assignment, the more he or she will be likely to engage in noncompliant behavior when presented with an aversive task (Cipani, 1998).

Often times, teachers employ reduction strategies to respond to noncompliant behavior once it occurs thus omitting to re-arrange the antecedents (i.e., classroom environment and instructional format) that occasion noncompliance. Such aversive techniques, though often effective in decreasing noncompliance on a short-term basis, do not usually result in increased compliance long-term and may eventually escalate to enhanced and maintained forms of noncompliance and teacher-student confrontations (Belfiore et al, 2008). Therefore, attempting to increase compliance as opposed to decrease noncompliance may serve as a more effective strategy towards managing behavior (Lee, 2005). Applied behavioral research has demonstrated that antecedent-based techniques designed to increase compliance have resulted in an increase in academic time, a decrease in time required to complete an assigned task, and have advanced positive learning experiences in students (Belfiore et al., 2008). Hence, a modification of the antecedents that occasion noncompliance serves as a preventive measure towards the occurrence of noncompliance while resulting in longer-lasting positive gains for the student (Lee, 2005).

Discussion

The educational system is not only expecting absolute obedience from teachers (i.e., "teachers' failure of 'performativity' could result in adverse consequences," *Performance, 2.3.1*) and other educational personnel [i.e., "the employment of principals and teachers (and system administrators) is conditional upon improving performance on system wide tests of student learning," *Monitoring, 2.3.3*], but also from students. "The state commands 'what is to be taught, when it is to be taught, and increasingly, how is it to be taught'" (*Performance, 2.3.1*). Deviation is deemed as noncompliant behavior. "Engaging in more enjoyable activity" becomes the equivalent of misbehavior.

Similarly to teachers who experience adverse consequences if they fail to submit to educational expectations (i.e., "teachers' failure of 'performativity' could result in adverse consequences," *Performance, 2.3.1*), students are punished (i.e. "reduction strategies") if they choose not to comply with educational methods, further enhancing the power over their lives and the achievement of the goal of corporate profit via the dissolution of spirituality. The contradictory to research findings "reduction strategies" implemented by teachers and parents in response to children's noncompliant behavior exemplify the power of conditioning to the destructive values and methods of the educational system.

2.17 Praise

Teachers have utilized verbal and physical praise in school settings as an intervention for "acknowledging appropriate behavior" (Blaze et al., 2014). Praising children for their creative endeavors may not always serve children's best interests. Yet, a number of teachers may perceive such "contention hard to swallow." Kohn suggests that excessive praise contributes to children craving adult attention and approval, depriving them from the experience of self-determination. In other words, repetitive praise causes children to become engaged in constantly pleasing the adult at the expense of being interested in the activity being praised for. Furthermore, praise is one means albeit not the only one, that can compromise children's creativity.

The assumption that children are not well equipped to conduct self-assessment underlines praise. Yet, research "contradicts this assumption." Glazer (2007) showed that 8-year-old children and children older than 8 years of age perceived praise given by an adult as lacking genuineness, particularly when used overwhelmingly. Other children reported that while teachers may praise their work, the tone of their voice communicates disappointment instead (Geist & Hohn, 2009). A study conducted by Elwell and Tiberio

(1994) further demonstrated that 54% of secondary-level students "preferred not being praised at all," 37% reported a preference for quiet praise while 9% enjoyed loud teacher praise as a consequence of "appropriate behavior" (Blaze et al., 2014).

According to researchers, teachers ought to engage in encouraging children's creative work rather praising it. While praise focuses children's attention on the teacher's evaluation of their creativity, encouragement allows them to "feel the pride in their own accomplishments" (Geist & Hohn, 2009).

2.18 Reward and Punishment

Alfie Kohn (1993) found that rewarding and punishing children, including using grades, "actually interfere with student learning." He further cites studies demonstrating that all elementary, high school and university students performed better on tasks when not rewarded compared to students rewarded for their accomplishment on assignments. According to Krishnamurti, punishing and rewarding children for purposes of control contributes to compulsion and prevents students from developing their intelligence and experiencing freedom. An educational approach of rewards and punishment further "becomes a game where students try to please the teacher" while forming a "social structure which is competitive, antagonistic and ruthless." Mutual respect and affection starting with the teacher instead of compulsion and discipline characterize the right kind of education. Mutual respect and affection can only emerge in an atmosphere of no fear. Being free of fear contributes to wisdom and the development of deep creative intelligence (Miller, 1999).

Discussion

The theory of Emotional Intelligence postulates that "every leader's main obligation is to... 'prime good feelings in those they lead' which in turn will generate the best behavior in others" (*Emotional Intelligence, 2.10*). With a focus on extrinsic motivation (i.e., "extrinsically-motivated individuals do not engage in an activity resulting out of personal interest, but rather 'for the consequence it is thought to be instrumentally linked to,'" *Motivation, 1.6*) instead of intrinsic motivation (i.e., "intrinsic motivation is consistently the most beneficial form of motivation for students' achievement...viewed as the prototype of autonomy," *Motivation, 1.6*), praise and reward appear to represent methods utilized by the educational system to manufacture unnatural positive emotions in students which ensure compliance with the expectations of the corporate agenda.

Furthermore and in striking similarity to standardized assessments, school work, fear appeals and the removal of subjects not addressed by NCLB, praise and reward lead to the exact opposite of what the educational system deceivingly propagates – academic failure and not academic achievement.

2.19 Technology

"Virtual worlds are becoming epidemic" (Lang, 2003). "There is widespread...support for the value of computers in educational settings and a political commitment to their introduction" (Plowman & Stephen, 2005). Online information is not only abundantly present, but growing exponentially and becoming obsolete every couple of years, begging "the questions, what are we teaching, and why" (Rushton, 2011)? Furthermore, children's perceptual and sense connection to the real world around them is a prerequisite for the development of abstract thought and critical thinking. Television or computers used in kindergartens are thus not capable of fostering the development of critical thinking skills later in life (Lang, 2003).

Discussion

Firmly focused on synthetic learning experiences, the cultivation of negative feelings, the withdrawal of superficial positive emotions and interaction with artificial intelligence, the educational system is compromising spirituality by replacing it with a virtual, programmable, predictable lower-consiousness reality. The seeming objective, in line with previous findings, is the prevention of "abstract thought and critical thinking," which ensures compliance with the corporate-profit driven educational agenda. "Online information…becoming obsolete every couple of years" while academic learning is becoming increasingly limited and standardized, provide additional validation of such conclusion.

2.20 Reading

Almost 40% of students in the U.S. struggle with learning to read. Reading instruction focused on systematic and explicit teaching of phonics and phonemic awareness, direct and indirect vocabulary instruction, guided oral reading as well as introduction to a number of reading comprehension strategies, have been suggested to improve the reading skills of struggling readers (Walsh et al., 2006).

Discussion

"In the USA today, education is brain-oriented; goals are cognitive, intellectual, and academic. We focus on the head, not the hands and heart" (*Pedagogy, 2.2*). Gardner further postulated that "teaching to only one or two kinds of intelligence, such as linguistic and logical-mathematical, is common but does not take advantage of students' potential." The high prevalence of U.S. students struggling with learning to read indicates that the implemented by mainstream education "brain-oriented" reading instruction is utterly ineffective, yet not accidental as previous findings demonstrated that academic achievement is a prefabricated goal.

2.21 Attention Deficit/Hyperactivity Disorder (ADHD)

In comparison to a teacher, "the artificial world created by interactive, high-definition video games...can be far more enticing... 'Michael, Michael are you there?' Mom yells upstairs, knowing her child has been classified as ADHD at school yet can't seem to pull himself away from the video game hour after hour at home" (Rushton, 2011).

***

"Attention deficit/hyperactivity disorder (ADHD) (APA, 2013) is described as "a neurodevelopmental disorder characterized by impairing levels of inattention, overactivity, and poor impulse control" (Sibley et al., 2014). Research findings revealed that "ADHD increases the likelihood of other psychiatric diagnoses" such as oppositional defiant disorder (ODD), conduct disorder (CD) and learning disorders (Hillard et al., 2013). "The onset of ADHD may occur as early as 3 years of age" (Gold et al., 2014). Approximately 8%-10% of school-age children are affected by ADHD (Narine et al., 2013). "A scientific and public debate is ongoing regarding the question of whether ADHD is overdiagnosed in children" (Bruchmuller et al., 2012).

"Historically characterized as a childhood disorder, it is now well accepted that ADHD afflicts adolescents and adults." It is estimated to affect between 5% and 10% of adolescents. Academic performance is at the forefront of "critically impaired" domains experienced by adolescents with ADHD. In comparison with adolescents without ADHD, adolescents with ADHD complete fewer academic assignments, perform poorer on standardized tests, receive lower grades, are more likely to be late or absent from classes and be suspended for disciplinary reasons. High rates of high school dropout due to course failure are also common in adolescents with ADHD. Statistical findings reveal up to 38% high school dropout rate of adolescents with ADHD. Academic difficulties, characteristic of students with ADHD, begin during the childhood years, appearing to "escalate at the transition to secondary school" (Sibley et al., 2014).

2.21.1 Treatment

The medications prescribed to children diagnosed with ADHD include psychostimulants, antidepressants, alpha-adrenergic agents and bupropion (Brown & La Rosa, 2002). "The rate of treatment with medication for patients with ADHD has been increasing since 2008." More than 2 million children with ADHD in the U.S. are "being treated with stimulants" (Gold et al., 2014). Psychostimulant consumption in Australia increased eight times and a half between 1994 and 2000.

Psychostimulants "increase the arousal level of the central nervous system (CNS) by stimulating the release and inhibiting the reuptake of the dopamine and noreadrenaline neurotransmitters," leading to increased attention and decreased gross motor activity and impulsiveness. Psychostimulants "have not been extensively researched through cortical measures such as electroencephalogram (EEG) coherence" (Dupuy et al., 2010). Short-term cognitive and academic improvement following stimulant medication treatment of ADHD "are well documented," yet long-term effects "are not yet well documented."

"The short-term adverse events associated with stimulants can be very harsh for patients and their families" (Ibrahim & Donyai, 2014). The possible short-term side effects of psychostimulant medications include insomnia, nausea, anorexia, anxiety, nightmares, blood pressure fluctuations, abdominal pain and weepiness while possible long-term side effects include cardiovascular dysfunction, weight loss, height suppression, drug dependence and drug abuse. Psychostimulants "may exacerbate existing tics, or they may precipitate tics or Tourette's syndrome, or a family history of Tourette's syndrome" (Brown & La Rosa, 2002). Research findings show a possible association between "using stimulants and reduced growth of children with ADHD" (Ibrahim & Donyai, 2014).

The psychostimulant Methylphenidate (MPH) is the main treatment medication for ADHD (Dupuy et al., 2010). The U.S. FDA has approved Adderall (dextroamphetamine/amphetamine), a psychostimulant, for the treatment of ADHD. It is "usually well tolerated," yet has common neurocognitive and psychiatric side effects such as "loss of appetite, insomnia, abdominal pain, weight loss, headache, nausea, anxiety, and nervousness." One "unusual" side effect of Adderall is trichotillomania (hair-pulling). Other "rare" neuropsychiatric side effects include aggressive behavior, mood changes and escalating irritability (Narine et al., 2013). Research findings further raise "the possibility that Adderall could decrease creativity in people using it for cognitive enhancement" (Farah et al., 2009).

Tricyclic antidepressants (TCAs) are the second leading choice for the "management of ADHD in children" who fail to respond to psychostimulant medications. "Their mechanism of action in ADHD is unknown." Sedation, constipation, drowsiness, insomnia, nightmares, blurred vision, dry mouth and seizures are adverse effects associated with TCAs (Brown & La Rosa, 2002).

Discussion

The symptoms of ADHD are strikingly parallel to the behaviors associated with noncompliance. Inattention as part of ADHD can be equated to "ignoring the teacher's request" in noncompliance, over-activity - with "engaging in more enjoyable activity" and poor impulse control - with "getting out of seat." Also in similarity to noncompliance, ADHD may lead to "more serious disruptive and delinquent behaviors" and "impede children's academic success." Lastly, harmful treatment interventions (i.e., "reduction strategies" for noncompliant behavior, *Noncompliance, 2.16*; ADHD medication), designed to increase compliance with the corporate-profit educational agenda, are implemented for both noncompliance and ADHD.

Since both noncompliance and ADHD share analogous symptoms, outcomes and treatment modalities, ADHD could be interpreted as an alternative to noncompliance name assigned to the failure of meeting imposed by the educational system expectations. The increasing rate of ADHD and the ongoing "scientific and public debate" in regards to the possibility of over-diagnosing ADHD in children raises the question as to whether noncompliance is being substituted by an ADHD diagnosis. The validity of such question is supported by findings in regards to subjects not addressed by NCLB being steadily removed prior to the enactment of NCLB and radically eradicated thereafter (i.e. desensitization).

Moreover, it was earlier demonstrated that one of the purposes of academic achievement is to conceal the actual educational objective of extinguishing spirituality. The finding that the only assigned beneficial outcome of ADHD medications is "short-term cognitive and academic improvement" while the side effects are drastic, provides additional support for such conclusion. On a similar note, as with praise and reward withdrawing virtual positive emotions in students, psychostimulants unnaturally induce the release of dopamine responsible for "increased attention and decreased gross motor activity and impulsiveness." Alternatively stated, students are forced into experiencing artificially-induced state of well-being as a means to meeting the expectations of the educational agenda, which, by implication, compromises spirituality.

Last, but not least, ADHD medications are: a) vastly prescribed to children despite the fact that they "have not been extensively researched;" b) U.S. FDA-approved (i.e., Adderall); c) leading to "short-term cognitive and academic improvement;" d) characterized by "not yet well documented" long-term effects and adverse side effects. Such findings not only provide further support for the conclusion that academic achievement serves the purpose of concealing the actual educational objective of extinguishing spirituality through harm, but reveal that U.S. FDA also personifies and executes the corporate-profit agenda executed via the dissolution of spirituality.

2.22 Marital Conflict

Marital conflict (i.e., physical and verbal aggression) has been linked to stress-related poor physiological, developmental and cognitive functioning in children. At the same time, studies have shown that children's "conduct problems and dysregulated externalizing behaviors were predictive of increased future marital conflict and probability of divorce (Hinnant et al., 2013).

Discussion

Research findings provide additional support for the power of projection and internalization of projected inner states.

2.23 Substance Abuse

"Risky drinking is a significant problem among undergraduate students, many of whom exhibit high rates of alcohol consumption." Heavy alcohol consumption amongst undergraduate students is associated with health and academic problems and is a predictor of the development of alcoholism. "Stress is one of the most likely contributing factors." Higher education students "experience elevated levels of stress related to new time demands, greater workload, financial strain and examinations" and report greater alcohol consumption during heightened stress periods (Magrys & Olmstead, 2015). The incentive salience theory explains drug addiction as the tolerance developed towards the rewarding consequence of drugs (Abraham et al., 2014).

Discussion

The "unwanted, intrusive thoughts, images, and impulses...reported by 80% to 90% of the general population...are normally evoked by external stimuli, stressful situations and negative emotional states" (*Uncomfortable Thoughts and Emotions, 2.14*). "Teachers' failure of 'performativity' could result in adverse consequences, including...chronic stress (*Performance, 2.5.1*) while "academic examinations and school work are considered to be the most stressful events of adolescent's life" (*Test Anxiety, 2.15.1*). Finally, educational system-induced "stress is one of the most likely contributing factors" of "heavy alcohol consumption amongst undergraduate students." Stress is hence a deliberately manufactured outcome of educational discourse.

It is further of little surprise that undergraduate and higher education students engage in "heavy alcohol consumption;" mainstream education cultivates negative emotional states and conditions students to unnaturally evoked rewarding experiences. The educational system is hence directly responsible for the "development of alcoholism" among higher education students.

2.24 Aggression and School Violence

More than 80% of people engage in aggression (i.e., "behavior directed toward individual with the intent to harm") over their lifespan. Aggression causes harm not only to the victim, but also to the perpetrator. "Billions of dollars in productivity are lost yearly due to aggression and its consequences." Homicide is the second leading cause of death among individuals between 15 and 24 years of age (Kulper et al., 2015).

"School violence is a widespread...phenomenon all over the world" (Berkowitz & Benbenishty, 2012). "School violence is at pandemic proportions." 2.7 million violent crimes take place at or in proximity to school on an annual basis while 11% of all teachers report being the subject of student victimization.

A review of 66 studies identified the following risk factors for school violence: individual (i.e., hyperactivity; internalizing disorders; problems with concentration; aggressiveness; "beliefs and attitudes favorable to deviant or antisocial behavior"), family (i.e., parental criminal behavior; child maltreatment; parents favoring violence; poor parent-child relationship), school (i.e., academic failure; withdrawal from school; "low bonding to school;" truancy), peer-related (i.e., gang involvement; "delinquent siblings"), community and neighborhood (i.e., delinquent neighborhood adults; poverty; exposure to violence; "community disorganization").

"To prevent violent and undesirable behaviors, it is necessary to deal with the underlying causes of these behaviors rather than merely creating deterrents or enforcing punishments." A common reason for academic disengagement revolves around students' perception that "academic success has little value in terms of meeting one's goals." The solution to disengagement with academics (associated with school violence) is to either prevent such disengagement or increase engagement. One way of doing so is "fostering a 'change from baseline' approach to evaluation rather than a norm-referenced orientation." A number of students compare their academic performance to that of top-performing students, "consistently falling short and thus experiencing consistently negative outcomes...competitive grading schemes (such as curving) and norm referenced assessments tend to exacerbate the issue." Encouraging students to evaluate their performance on the basis of their own growth rather in comparison to others' and appropriately increasing the difficulty of tasks will facilitate positive perception of personal performance (Osborne, 2004). A positive school climate may also serve as a protective factor against student engagement in aggressive behavior (Klein et al., 2012).

2.25 Peer Victimization

In the past decade and a half, peer victimization (i.e., bullying) "has become...often neglected problem in schools around the world" (Cornell et al., 2013). Relational peer victimization, the act of "manipulating or threatening to damage the victim's relationship" as a means to cause harm, is prevalent among children in early grades. Kochenderfer & Ladd (1996) demonstrated that 42% of kindergarten students were exposed to relational victimization to some extent while 15% experienced drastic rates of relational peer victimization. There is evidence to suggest that "negative peer interactions" in the early grades predict "under-achievement and unemployment at age 18." Relational peer victimization contributes to stress, which may deplete "cognitive resources" necessary for learning "new educational material" (Valiente et al., 2014).

2.26 Dating Violence

Between 2010 and 2011, approximately 1.1 million people were victimized by the person's intimate partner (Milaniak & Widom, 2014). There are between 400,000 and 900,000 victims of teen dating violence (TDV) in the United States (Hamby et al., 2012).

Discussion

Child maltreatment is identified as a major risk factor for school violence. Hence, mainstream education is accountable for the epidemic rates of school violent behavior. Specifically, "the increasing standardization of learning prepares young people to act aggressively...It contributes little or nothing to decent communities, loving relationships, or ways to transcend self-centeredness" (*Standardization, 2.3.2*). In other words, it is not coincidental that "unwanted, intrusive thoughts, images, and impulses are reported by 80% to 90% of the general population" (*Uncomfortable Thoughts and Emotions, 2.14*), over 80% of people engage in acts of aggression over the duration of their lifespan while aggression, violence and victimization are prominent amongst youth. It was earlier suggested that "emotions trigger the imagination which, in combination with cognition, establishes the basis for experiencing reality. Feelings derived from imagination 'can be systematic in producing behavior'" (*Personal Identity, 1.3.1.1*). Via the cultivation of negative affect (i.e., fear) and the removal of opportunities for positive emotions, the educational system creates a low vibration experiential space which, through the power of projection, triggers aggressive behavior.

2.27 Failure to Graduate and School Dropout

1.3 million American high school students did not graduate from high school in 2010, resulting in $336 million in economic losses. Academic performance, family, demographic and individual variables are described as risk for the failure to graduate high school factors, yet "there is no single cause for failure to graduate." Research demonstrates that children who exhibit disruptive behaviors (i.e., aggressive; oppositional; hyperactive-inattentive) in the early grades are more likely to fail to complete high school (Lynch et al., 2014).

Moreover, about 1.3 million students drop out of high school in the U.S. alone each year. "School dropout is better understood as a process of disengagement from school rather than a sudden event" (Cornell et al., 2013).

Discussion

It was earlier demonstrated that school tests and assignments resulted in anxiety which is "one of the main factors leading to low academic performance" and subsequent failure to graduate from high school. Aggression, a risk factor associated with failure to graduate, was also found to correlate with educational methods. Lastly, "school dropout" is "better understood as a process of disengagement from school rather than a sudden event" (*Cognitive Intelligence, 2.9*). "A common reason for academic disengagement revolves around students' perception that "academic success has little value in terms of meeting one's goals" (*Aggression and School Violence, 2.24*). There is also a "greater likelihood that children would 'disengage' from a learning task if they believe that intelligence is fixed and their performance on a learning task is negatively evaluated" (*Cognitive Intelligence, 2.9*). Hence, the educational system bears direct responsibility for the epidemic rates of failure to graduate and school dropout.

2.28 Suicide

Global suicide rates are higher in urban compared to rural areas and among men compared to women (Jianlin, 2000). On average, 85 Americans commit suicide each day. (Antai-Otong, 2003). Suicide (39,518 deaths, 78% of whom were men) was the 10th leading cause of death in the U.S. in 2011 (Granato et al., 2014). The highest rate of committed suicide is among white men 85 years of age and older.

"Youth Suicide is a significant health problem among youth in society" (Antai-Otong, 2003). According to data generated by the Center for Disease Control and Prevention (2013), suicide in the U.S. "is the third leading cause of death for young people 10 to 24 years old, with over 157,000 attempts per year" (Tynan, 2013). Center for Disease and Control (2009) survey findings revealed 14% of American high-school students contemplated suicide while 6% reported having attempted suicide (Klimes-Dougan et al., 2013). The Center for Disease Control and Prevention (2013) further reported that 12.5% of adolescent boys and 19.3% of adolescent girls "seriously considered suicide" while 5.8% of adolescent boys and 9.8% of adolescent girls made a suicide attempt (Wintersteen & Diamond, 2013).

Risk factors for suicide include unemployment, low income, being single, retired, disabled, family history of mental illness and/or suicide and absence from work due to sickness (Sinclair et al., 2005). The most common mental illnesses associated with worldwide suicide are depression, personality disorder and alcoholism (Antai-Otong, 2003). 50% of people who have committed suicide have suffered from depression (Van Praag, 2002). Immature coping skills and ego functioning represent risk factors for suicide among children and adolescents (Antai-Otong, 2003).

Discussion

Test anxiety is "one of the main factors leading to low academic performance...20% of students experiencing test anxiety withdraw from school prior to graduation as a result of 'repeated academic failure...' Students who fail to graduate with a high school diploma...are...not as likely to be employed or to earn as much as graduates do" (*Test Anxiety, 2.15.1*). If unemployment and low income are risk factors for suicide, it follows that test anxiety, a direct outcome of educational approaches, is also a risk factor for suicide. Similarly, educational methods are directly correlated to alcoholism (a different risk factor for suicide) amongst higher education students.

The finding that "suicide in the U.S. 'is the third leading cause of death for young people 10 to 24 years old, with over 157,000 attempts per year'" while "immature coping skills...represent" a risk factor "for suicide among children and adolescents" is further not accidental. The primary focus of mainstream education is teaching limited subjects addressed by NCLB and not on coping with the adverse effects of its methods (i.e., confined learning opportunities; test anxiety; fear appeals; praise and reward). Therefore, immature coping skills as a risk factor for suicide are also directly associated with educational methods.

2.29 Unemployment, Crime and Drugs

As the handmaiden of the American political economy, the school system has helped to divide our cities. It has saddled many citizens with massive unemployment and a dependence on crime and drugs. This division is the focus for most educational policymaking, and it disrupts daily life in all our classrooms" (McDermott, 1992).

***

"The average educational level of the labor force ages 25 and older has increased over the years, and the unemployment rate has trended downward over the past two decades" (De Prince, Jr. & Morris, 2008). Downsizing "has become a normal practice in many countries." Freeman and Cameron (1993) define downsizing as "an intentional management action involving a reduction in workforce and designed to improve a company's competitive position." More than 6.5 million jobs were lost in the U.S. since the recession in December, 2007 due to downsizing. This number is expected to continue to grow. Asian countries such as South Korea, Japan, China and Taiwan have also been affected by "significant employee reductions" (Long, 2013).

Discussion

Academic achievement requires unequivocal compliance with mainstream educational practices, integration of knowledge and skills acquired through the academic curriculum and suppression of spirituality. The high prevalence of unemployment reveals that students who renounce their own well-being or spirituality in exchange for gaining "access to...rewards" (*Sorting, 2.6*) are deceived into believing that their inhumane efforts guarantee a status on the economical hierarchical ladder. Such students are no longer of service to corporations (i.e., downsizing) once the "new kinds of...creative capital" leading to companies reaping "ideas and innovation" (*Creativity Re-Defined, 2.5*), result in corporate, not shared, profit. Absolute corporate profit is acquired when "the American education system...sorts each new generation into approximately the same configuration as the previous generation" (*Sorting, 2.6*). Hence, through all academic achievement, crime and drugs, spirituality in humanity is compromised while the goal of mainstream education, namely corporate profit, is achieved.

2.30 Work Victimization

According to findings from a survey, 37% of employees in the U.S. or 54 million people have experienced victimization at work. 45% of victimized employees reported compromised health as a result of the associated with the victimization stress (Yamada et al., 2014).

Discussion

"The increasing standardization of learning prepares young people to act aggressively…in the job market and the competitive corporate world" (*Standardization, 2.3.2*). The epidemic rate of work victimization in the U.S. is thus directly correlated with mainstream educational methods and its goal of corporate profit achieved through compromised well-being.

2.31 Earth

"Health is a quality of the organism, including its relations with other organisms and their shared habitat…Healthy humans cannot exist without a healthy biosphere. It is our home…The ultimate truth is that the human species is utterly dependent on the biosphere for its survival."

   The deterioration of earth and the concentration of profit and power in the hands of corporations affect all human beings. An increasing number of people currently "have tremendous power, amplified by sophisticated technologies, to manipulate, control, alter, and seriously damage the biosphere. But because they are disconnected from the natural world…they do not seem to have the ethical or spiritual sensitivity to use this power wisely, sparingly, or for the good of the whole. The newly acquired power to manipulate genetics, consciousness, information and communication "ultimately touches every one of us, often in deeply troubling ways." Corporations manipulate the genetic code of plants and add chemicals to food to increase their shelf-life "for the sake of greater profits. And everything happens faster, and faster still...We are permanently reducing the ecological quality of the planet at an unprecedented rate, to the point of destroying whole ecosystems containing thousands of species not yet discovered." A "monoculture" of advertisement, stock market news, celebrities and sports "trivial gossip" is "now spreading around the planet" in rapid ways. Historically, humanity engaged in tangible activities (i.e., agriculture) providing "meaning...and vital connections to the world." In contrast, "in this emerging postmodern society," millions spend their time engaging with a computer screen.

"Now we need to ask why these new powers are not being used on behalf of all humanity and to preserve the sanctity of life on earth, but primarily to help those who are already excessively wealthy and powerful become obscenely wealthy and powerful. The arrival of this brave new world, this 'new world order,' compels us to make a fundamental moral decision: Shall we continue to celebrate, indeed worship, the utilitarian, manipulative style of thinking that made global industrialization possible?...Is it possible that it might be a tremendously destructive mistake to continue to treat the world entirely as a resource, as fuel for the omnivorous economic machine we have built" (Miller, 2001)?

"If we are to save our planet, we need to develop a new common sense that features persons, not only in relation to each other but in relation to the wider universe" (McDermott, 1992). The Cosmos or "the universe is not merely a vast collection of stars and galaxies that we can study through telescopes, but an interconnected whole that encompasses everything that exists and everything that *can* exist" (Miller, 2001). We have recently started to realize that "we are killing the planet." The human race is before "environmental changes that are threatening existence as we know it." We are to either "regain awareness of who we are as humans and our relationship with the environment" or face "'icebergs' from which there is no escape...Our education is still preparing young people for our past and not their future," preparing students "for an economy that does not see the environment as essential to our existence, that ignores the 'icebergs' ahead... jeopardizing the lives of our children and their children." The notion of human beings dominating nature is being questioned and replaced by the realization that Earth is a living being and we are part of nature, dependent on the environment for our survival. Such new notion is "challenging us to live in an ecologically sound way and to develop an approach to education that cultivates the heart as well as the mind, inspires cooperation rather than competition, empathy and love instead of violence and hate" (Greenberg, 2011). "Love should not be underestimated as a significant developmental and evolutionary force" (Gidley, 2007). Love and compassion "are the basic elements supporting our life and happiness" (Sullivan et al., 2010). "The new story needs to be told. Where are the storytellers" (Greenberg, 2011)? "Children are the revolutionary bridge, continuously rebuilding the connection between present and future states of planet Earth" (Moore, 1997).

Discussion

There is an undeniable similarity between mainstream educational and corporate leaders. Both are "disconnected from the natural world" and "do not seem to have the ethical or spiritual sensitivity to use...power wisely, sparingly, or for the good of the whole." Adding the fact that the goal of the educational system is corporate profit while corporations obliterate the biosphere, engage in epidemic rates of downsizing, allow work victimization to take place and poison human beings "for the sake of greater profits" clearly indicates that both mainstream education and corporations are managed by individuals sharing the exact same value system of acquiring absolute profit via power over others or via the extinguishment of spirituality (life) on Earth. The destructive outcome of their projected creation is a direct reflection of the spirituality-devoid inner selves they embody.

References

Abraham, A. D., Neve, K. A. & Lattal, K. M. (2014). Dopamine and extinction: A convergence of theory with fear and reward circuitry. *Neurobiology of Learning and Memory, 108,* 65-77.

Allam, C. (2008). Creative activity and its impact on student learning – issues of implementation. *Innovations in Education and Teaching International, 45*(3), 281-288.

Almon, J. Educating for creative thinking: The Waldorf approach.

Antai-Otong, D. (2003). Suicide: Life span considerations. *Nursing Clinics of North America, 38,* 137-150.

Belfiore, P. J., Basile, S. P., Lee, D. L. (2008). Using high probability command sequence to increase classroom compliance: The role of behavioral momentum. *Journal of Behavioral Education, 17*(2), 160-171.

Bellipanni, K. D., Tingstrom, D. H., Olmi, D. J. & Roberts, D. S. (2013). The sequential introduction of positive antecedent and consequent components in a compliance training package with elementary students. *Behavior Modification, 37*(6) 768-789.

Berkowitz, R. & Benbenishty, R. (2012). Perceptions of teachers' support, safety, and absence from school because of fear among victims, bullies, and bully-victims. *American Journal of Orthopsychiatry*, *82*(1), 67-74.

Blaze, J. T., Olmi, D. J., Mercer, S. H., Dufrene, B. A. & Tingstom, D. H. (2014). Loud versus quiet praise: A direct behavioral comparison in secondary classrooms. *Journal of School Psychology*, *52*, 349-360.

Braddock, L. (2011). Psychological identification, imagination and psychoanalysis. *Philosophical Psychology*, *24*(5), 639-657.

Brown, R. T. & La Rosa, A. (2002). Recent developments in the pharmacotherapy of Attention-Deficit/Hyperactivity Disorder (ADHD). *Professional Psychology: Research and Practice*, *33*(6), 591-595.

Bruchmuller, K., Margraf, J. & Schneider, S. (2012). Is ADHD diagnosed in accord with diagnostic criteria? Overdiagnosis and influence of client gender on diagnosis. *Journal of Consulting and Clinical Psychology*, *80*(1), 128-138.

Burnard, P. & White, J. (2008). Creativity and performativity: Counterpoints in British and Australian education. *British Educational Research Journal*, *34*(5), 667-682.

Buss, K. A. (2011). Which fearful toddlers should we worry about? Context, fear regulation, and anxiety risk. *Developmental Psychology*, *47*(3), 804-819.

Camargo-Figuera, F. A., Barros, A. JD, Santos, I. S., Matijasevich, A. & Barros, F. C. (2014). Early life determinants of low IQ at age 6 in children from the 2004 Pelotas Birth Cohort: A predictive approach. *BMC Pediatrics*, *14*(308), 1-12.

Carrington, P. R. & Kratochwill, T. R. (1994). Behavioral consultation with parents: Using competency-based training to modify child noncompliance. *School Psychology Review*, *23*(4), 669-693.

Chaudhary, B. & Aswal, M. (2013). Imparting spiritual intelligence curriculum in our classrooms. *European Academic Research, 1*(7), 1508-1515.

Cipani, E. (1998). Three behavioral functions of classroom noncompliance: Diagnostic and treatment implications. *Focus on Autism and Other Developmental Disabilities, 13*(2), 66-72.

Claxton, G. (2006). Thinking at the edge: Developing soft creativity. *Cambridge Journal of Education, 36*(3), 351-362.

Clegg, P. (2008). Creativity and critical thinking in the globalised university. *Innovations in Education and Teaching International, 45*(3), 219-226.

Cohen, M. & Khalaila, R. (2014). Saliva pH as a biomarker of exam stress and a predictor of exam performance. *Journal of Psychosomatic Research, 77*, 420-425.

Cornell, D., Gregory, A., Huang, F. & Fan, X. (2013). Perceived prevalence of teasing and bullying predicts high school dropout rates. *Journal of Educational Psychology, 105*(1), 138-149.

Corrigan, P. T. (2010). Spirituality and literary studies. *ENCOUNTER: Education for Meaning and Social Justice, 23*(4), 47-51.

Craft, A. (2006). Fostering creativity with wisdom. *Cambridge Journal of Education, 36*(3), 337-350.

Craft, A. & Jeffrey, B. (2008). Creativity and performativity in teaching and learning: Tensions, dilemmas, constraints, accommodations and synthesis. *British Educational Research Journal, 34*(5), 577-584.

Croxford, L. & David Raffe, D. (2013). Differentiation and social segregation of UK higher education, 1996-2010. *Oxford Review of Education, 39*(2), 172-192.

Cupit, C. G. (2007). The marriage of science and spirit: Dynamic systems theory and the development of spirituality. *International Journal of Children's Spirituality, 12*(2), 105-116.

Denham, S. A., Bassett, H. H. & Zinsser, K. (2012). Early childhood teachers as socializers of young children's emotional competence. *Early Childhood Education Journal, 40*, 137-143.

De Prince, Jr., A. E. & Morris, P. D. (2008). The effects of education on the natural rate of unemployment. *Business Economics*, 45-54.

D'Mello, S. (2013). A selective meta-analysis on the relative incidence of discrete affective states during learning with technology. *Journal of Educational Psychology, 105*(4), 1082-1099.

Dupuy, F. E., Clarke, A. R., Barry, R. J., McCarthy, R. & Selikowitz, M. (2010). EEG coherence in children with attention-deficit/hyperactivity disorder: Differences between good and poor responders to methylphenidate. *Psychiatry Research, 180*, 114-119.

Fairbrother, N., Barr, R. G., Pauwels, J., Brant, R. & Green, J. (2014). Maternal thoughts of harm in response to infant crying: An experimental analysis. *Archives of Women's Mental Health*, 1-9.

Farah, M. J., Haimm, C., Sankoorikal, G. & Chatterjee, A. (2009). When we enhance cognition with Adderall, do we sacrifice creativity? A preliminary study. *Psychopharmacology, 202*, 541-547.

Galla, B. M., Plummer, B. D., White, R. E., Meketon, D., D'Mello, S. & Duckworth, A. L. (2014). The Academic Diligence Task (ADT): Assessing individual differences in effort on tedious but important schoolwork. *Contemporary Educational Psychology, 39*, 314-325.

Gardner, H. & Moran, S. (2006). The science of multiple intelligences theory: A response to Lynn Waterhouse. *Educational Psychologist, 41*(4), 227-232.

Geist, E. & Hohn, J. (2009). Encouraging creativity in the face of administrative convenience: How our schools discourage divergent thinking. *Education, 130*(1), 141-150.

Gidley, J. M. (2010). Holistic education and visions of rehumanized futures. *Research on Steiner Education, 1*(2), 139-147.

Gold, M. S., Blum, K., Oscar-Berman, M. & Braverman, E. R. (2014). Low dopamine function in Attention Deficit/Hyperactivity Disorder: Should genotyping signify early diagnosis in children? *Postgraduate Medicine, 126*(1), 153-177.

Goral, M. (2010). Teacher support and revival in Waldorf-inspired classrooms. *ENCOUNTER: Education for Meaning and Social Justice, 23*(2), 53-58.

Granato, S. L., Smith, P. N. & Selwyn, C. N. (2014). Acquired capability and masculine gender norm adherence: Potential pathways to higher rates of male suicide. *Psychology of Men & Masculinity*, 1-8.

Greenberg, A. (2011). Education and the new story of human existence. *ENCOUNTER: Education for Meaning and Social Justice, 24*(1), 45-47.

Gurr, D. A review of school accountability in Australia. 1-18.

Hamby, S., Finkelhor, D. & Turner, H. (2012). Teen dating violence: Co-occurrence with other victimizations in the National Survey of Children's Exposure to Violence (NatSCEV). *Psychology of Violence, 2*(2), 111-124.

Hargreaves, J. (2008). Risk: The ethics of creative curriculum. *Innovations in Education and Teaching International, 45*(3), 227-234.

Hillard, B., El-Baz, A. S., Sears, L., Tasman, A. & Sokhadze, E. M. (2013). Neurofeedback training aimed to improve focused attention and alertness in children with ADHD: A study of relative power of EEG rhythms using custom-made software application. *Clinical EEG and Neuroscience, 44*(3), 193-202.

Hinnant, J. B., El-Sheikh, M., Keiley, M. & Buckhalt, J. A. (2013). Marital conflict, allostatic load, and the development of children's fluid cognitive performance. *Child Development, 84*(6), 2003-2014.

Horsley, S. (2009). The politics of public accountability: Implications for centralized music education policy development and implementation. *Arts Education Policy Review, 110*(4), 6-12.

Humphries, C. A., Bidner, S. & Edwards, C. (2011). Integrated learning with physical education and music. *The Clearing House, 84*, 174-179.

Hunt, H. T. (2012). A collective unconscious reconsidered: Jung's archetypal imagination in the light of contemporary psychology and social science. *Journal of Analytical Psychology, 57*, 76-98.

Ibrahim, K. & Donyai, P. (2014). Drug holidays from ADHD medication: International experience over the past four decades. *Journal of Attention Disorders*, 1-18.

Jianlin, J. (2000). Suicide rates and mental health services in modern China. *Crisis, 21*(3), 118-121.

Jureidini, J. N. (2014). Let children cry. *Medical Journal of Australia, 201*(10), 612-613.

Kiviuori, J. & Salmi, V. (2009). The challenge of special needs education in school-based delinquency research. *Journal of Scandinavian Studies in Criminology and Crime Prevention, 10*, 2-17.

Klein, J., Cornell, D. & Konold, T. (2012). Relationships between bullying, school climate, and student risk behaviors. *School Psychology Quarterly, 27*(3), 154-169.

Klimes-Dougan, B., Klingbeil, D. A. & Meller, S. J. (2013). The impact of universal suicide-prevention programs on the help-seeking attitudes and behaviors of youths. *Crisis, 34*(2), 82-97.

Kulper, D. A., Kleiman, E. M., McCloskey, M. S., Berman, M. E. & Coccaso, E. F. (2015). The experience of aggressive outbursts in intermittent explosive disorder. *Psychiatry Research, 225*(3), 710-715.

Lang, P. (2003). The kindergarten child. *Association of Waldorf Schools of North America*, 13-16.

Lee, D. (2005). Increasing compliance: A quantitative synthesis of applied research on high-probability request sequences. *Exceptionality, 23*(3), 141-154.

Loia, D. & Dillon, P. (2006). Adaptive educational environments as creative spaces. *Cambridge Journal of Education, 36*(3), 363-381.

Long, J. (2013). Workplace pressure moderates perception of threat or opportunity and employee creativity after downsizing. *Social Behavior and Personality, 41*(6), 957-970.

Lynch, R. J., Kistner, J. A. & Allan, N. P. (2014). Distinguishing among disruptive behaviors to help predict high school graduation: Does gender matter? *Journal of School Psychology, 52*, 407-418.

Magrys, S. A. & Olmstead, M. C. (2015). Acute stress increases voluntary consumption of alcohol in undergraduates. *Alcohol and Alcoholism*, 1-6.

Mary, R. A., Marslin, G., Franklin, G. & Sheeba, C. J. (2014). Test anxiety levels of board exam going students in Tamil Nadu, India. *BioMed Research International*, 1-9.

McDermott, R. (1992). Waldorf education in America: A promise and its problems. *ReVision, 15*(2), 1-14.

Miele, D. B., Son, L. K. & Metcalfe, J. (2013). Children's naive theories of intelligence influence their metacognitive judgments. *Child Development, 84*(6), 1879-1886.

Milaniak, I. & Widom, C. Z. (2014). Does child abuse and neglect increase risk for perpetration of violence inside and outside the home? *Psychology of Violence*, 1-10.

Miller, J. P. (1999). Krishnamurti and holistic education. 1-20.

Miller, R. A brief history of alternative education. Retrieved from http://southerncrossreview.org/55/miller-education.htm

Miller, R. (2001). Making connections to the world some thoughts on holistic curriculum. *ENCOUNTER: Education for Meaning and Social Justice, 14*(4), 29-35.

Moore, C. R. (1997). The need for nature: A childhood right. *Social Justice, 24*(3), 203-220.

Mountain, V. (2007). Educational contexts for the development of children's spirituality: Exploring the use of imagination. *International Journal of Children's Spirituality, 12*(2), 191-205.

Narine, C., Sarwar, S. R. & Rais, T. B. (2013). Adderall-induced Trichotillomania: A case report. *Innovations in Clinical Neuroscience, 10*(7-8), 13-14.

Nicholson, D. W. (2000). Layers of experience: Forms of representation in a Waldorf school classroom. *Journal of Curriculum Studies, 32*(4), 575-587.

Orbach, G., Lindsay, S. & Grey, S. (2007). A randomised placebo-controlled trial of a self-help Internet-based intervention for test anxiety. *Behaviour Research and Therapy, 45*, 483-496.

Osborne, J. W. (2004). Identification with academics and violence in schools. *Review of General Psychology, 8*(3), 147-162.

Persellin, D. C. (2007). Policies, practices, and promises: Challenges to early childhood music education in the United States. *Arts Education Policy Review, 109*(2), 54-61.

Pijl, S. J., Frostad, P. & Flem, A. (2008). The social position of pupils with special needs in regular schools. *Scandinavian Journal of Educational Research, 52*(4), 387-405.

Plowman, L. & Stephen, C. (2005). Children, play, and computers in pre-school education. *British Journal of Educational Technology, 36*(2), 145-157.

Pollard, T. M., Steptoe, A., Canaan, L., Davies, G. J. & Wardle, J. (1995). Effect of academic examination stress on eating behavior and blood lipid levels. *International Journal of Behavioral Medicine, 2*(4), 299-320.

Pouris, A. & Inglesi-Lotz, R. (2014). The contribution of higher education institutions to the South African economy. *South African Journal of Science, 110*(3/4), 1-5.

Putwain, D. & Remedios, R. (2014). The scare tactic: Do fear appeals predict motivation and exam scores? *School Psychology Quarterly, 29*(4), 503-516.

Rafferty, Y. (2013). Child trafficking and commercial sexual exploitation: A review of promising prevention policies and programs. *American Journal of Orthopsychiatry, 83*(4), 559-575.

Rajiah, K. & Saravanan, C. (2014). The effectiveness of psychoeducation and systematic desensitization to reduce test anxiety among first-year pharmacy students. *American Journal of Pharmaceutical Education, 78*(9), 1-7.

Rushton, S. (2011). Neuroscience, early childhood education and play: We are doing it right! *Early Childhood Education Journal, 39*, 89-94.

Sibley, M. H., Altszuler, A. R., Morrow, A. S. & Merrill, B. M. (2014). Mapping the academic problem behaviors of adolescents with ADHD. *School Psychology Quarterly, 29*(4), 422-437.

Simmons, R. & Thompson, R. (2008). Creativity and performativity: The case of further education. *British Educational Research Journal, 34*(5), 601-618.

Sinclair, J. M. A., Harriss, L., Baldwin, D. S. & King, E. A. (2005). Suicide in depressive disorders: A retrospective case-control study of 127 suicides. *Journal of Affective Disorders, 87*, 107-113.

Spangler, G. (1997). Psychological and physiological responses during an exam and their relation to personality characteristics. *Psychoneuroendocrinology, 22*(6), 423-441.

Sobo, E. (2012). "This is Not Head-to-Head Education:" Whole child development in a Waldorf school. *Learning In and Out of School: Education across the Globe*, 1-25.

Strawn, J. R., Weldge, J. A., Wehry, A. M., Keeshin, B. & Rynn, M., A. (2014). Efficacy and tolerability of antidepressants in pediatric anxiety disorders: A systematic review and meta-analysis. *Depression and Anxiety, 00*, 1-9.

Sullivan, B. M., Wiist, B. & Wayment, H. (2010). The Buddhist health study: Meditation on love and compassion as features of religious practice. *Cross Currents*, 185-207.

Tynan, W. D. (2013). Suicide and youth: Challenges for the health care system. *Clinical Practice in Pediatric Psychology, 1*(3),289-290.

Valiente, C., Swanson, J., Lemery-Chalfant, K. & Berger, R. H. (2014). Children's effortful control and academic achievement: Do relational peer victimization and classroom participation operate as mediators? *Journal of School Psychology, 52*, 433-445.

Van Praag, H. M. (2002). Why has the antidepressant era not shown a significant drop in suicide rates? *Crisis, 23*(2), 77-82.

Vayalilkarottu, J. (2012). Holistic health and well-being: A psycho-spiritual/religious and theological perspective. *Asian Journal of Psychiatry, 5*, 347-350.

Wachelka, D. & Katz, R. C. (1999). Reducing test anxiety and improving academic self-esteem in high school and college students with learning disabilities. *Journal of Behavior Therapy and Experimental Psychiatry, 30*, 191-198.

Walsh, K., Glaser, D. & Wilcox, D. D. (2006). What education schools aren't teaching about reading and what elementary teachers aren't Learning. *National Council on Teacher Quality*, 1-83.

Waterhouse, L. (2006). Inadequate evidence for multiple intelligences, Mozart effect, and emotional intelligence theories. *Educational Psychologist, 41*(4), 247-255.

Wintersteen, M. B. & Diamond, G. S. (2013). Youth suicide prevention in primary care: A model program and its impact on psychiatric emergency referrals. *Clinical Practice in Pediatric Psychology, 1*(3), 295-305.

Yamada, S., Cappadocia, M. C. & Pepler, D. (2014). Workplace bullying in Canadian graduate psychology programs: Student perspectives of student–supervisor relationships. *Training and Education in Professional Psychology, 8*(1), 58-67.

Zachopouloua, E., Trevlasa, E., Konstadinidoub, E. & Archimedes Project Research Group (2006). The design and implementation of a physical education program to promote children's creativity in the early years. *International Journal of Early Years Education, 14*(3), 279-294.

Zaidell, D. W. (2014). Creativity, brain, and art: Biological and neurological considerations. *Frontiers in Human Neuroscience, 8*(389), 1-9.

Zhang, Z., Su, H., Peng, Q., Yang, Q. & Cheng, X. (2011). Exam anxiety induces significant blood pressure and heart rate increase in college students. *Clinical and Experimental Hypertension, 33*(5), 281-286.

Chapter 3

ALTERNATIVE AND HOLISTIC EDUCATION

3.1 Alternative Education

Those who worked for progressive, child-centered, or humanistic education within the system...have found little support for their vision in recent years, and many have turned to alternative settings."

***

Alternative and home schooling are the preferred methods of education by many people who view the "agenda of 'social efficiency'" as not conductive to values such as creativity, individuality, spiritual development and democracy. A number of alternative twentieth century schooling methods are rooted within the philosophy of three European philosophers and educators: Friedrich Froebel, Jean-Jacques Rousseau and Johann Heinrich. According to Rousseau, "education should follow the child's natural growth rather than the demands of society, which...tend to thwart all that is organic, natural and spiritual." Such "emphasis on the innate development of human nature became the primary philosophical basis for many alternative movements in education."

Alternative education grew exponentially during the 1960s (Miller). European-based research on Waldorf schools and a 2008 report by *Primary Review* (Cambridge) found that alternative educational methods, including Waldorf education and home schooling "produce better academic results" (Syringa Mountain School, 2013).

Discussion

In full accord with: a) the "resistance to creating new citizens with new minds" (*Pedagogy, 2.2*); b) the ignored "imperative to educate children with the evolution of consciousness in mind" in spite of the "advocacy of a number of educational researchers worldwide" (*Spiritual Intelligence, 2.11*); c) the fact that public schools have "fallen deeply into the job of sorting out those who will have access to the rewards of our culture from those who will not" despite "the efforts of millions of concerned teachers and administrators" (*Sorting, 2.6*); d) the finding that "spiritual development has been given lip service in much of the educational literature" (*Spiritual Intelligence, 2.11*); e) the fact that "studies" confirming a strong positive association between arts curriculum and academic achievement "have been ignored in mainstream education" (*Arts, 1.4*), "those who worked for progressive, child-centered, or humanistic education within the system...have found little support for their vision in recent years." Also in line with previous findings, such lack of support is present despite the finding that "alternative educational methods, including Waldorf education and home schooling "produce better academic results."

3.2 Holistic Education

According to Krishnamurti, "the highest function of education is to bring about an integrated individual who is capable of dealing with life as a whole" (Miller, 1999).

***

"In the 'serious business' of education and learning, squeezed on either side by the audit culture and high stakes testing, such concepts as laughter, play, dancing and happiness seem remote. It is encouraging to see these broad human literacies appearing at the post-formal table of educational offerings" (Gidley, 2007). "In the "postindustrial" or "postmodern" era that seem to be emerging now, the industrial-age model of "social efficiency" is possibly starting to become obsolete" (Miller).

Holistic education or the realization of the importance of education in "awakening new forms of consciousness" has surfaced in recent years (Gidley, 2007). Integral/holistic human development is pertinent to achieving a sustainable future" (Vayalilkarottu, 2012). According to holistic thought, each person embodies individual dreams, experiences, feelings and "each person reflects...a meaningful pattern of influences, actions, and thoughts that shape one's possibilities." Each child requires "the right kind of support, the right kind of environment" in order to unfold the possibilities pertinent to his or her developmental stage (Miller, 2001). According to holism, human life can be fulfilling only when the human experience is meaningful and when our sense of connecting to the world (i.e., to the biosphere; physical world; Cosmos; family, etc.) is re-established. "Holistic thought is an attempt to reclaim the sense of connection to the world that utilitarian manipulation and advanced technology have steadily eroded and now, by the dawn of the twenty-first century, nearly wiped out...Holistic education seeks to liberate students from the authoritarian system of behavior management that in the modern world we have come to call 'education'" (Miller, 2001). In his book, "Education and Spirituality," Ramon Gallegos Nava views spirituality as an integral part of holistic education (Chaudhary & Aswal, 2013).

Discussion

Results from a meta-analysis demonstrated that "participants in a negative mood had a tendency towards greater creativity on performance-based or serious creativity tasks compared to participants in a positive mood" (*Positive Mood, 1.8*). Such finding confirms the conclusion that "the 'serious businesses of education and learning" is orchestrated by individuals who choose negativity as their primary emotional state.

References

Chaudhary, B. & Aswal, M. (2013). Imparting spiritual intelligence curriculum in our classrooms. *European Academic Research, 1*(7), 1508-1515.

Gidley, J. M. (2007). Educational imperatives of the evolution of consciousness: The integral visions of Rudolf Steiner and Ken Wilber. *The International Journal of Children's Spirituality, 12*(2), 117-135.

Miller, J. P. (1999). Krishnamurti and holistic education. 1-20.

Miller, R. A brief history of alternative education. Retrieved from http://southerncrossreview.org/55/miller-education.htm

Miller, R. (2001). Making connections to the world some thoughts on holistic curriculum. *ENCOUNTER: Education for Meaning and Social Justice, 14*(4), 29-35.

Syringa Mountain School (2013). Syringa Mountain School: Cultivating the head, heart and hands. 1-122.

Vayalilkarottu, J. (2012). Holistic health and well-being: A psycho-spiritual/religious and theological perspective. *Asian Journal of Psychiatry, 5*, 347-350.

Chapter 4

WALDORF EDUCATION

"We need: an educational system that transforms our daily preoccupation with technique to an attention to spirit, that moves us from strategy to principle, from knowledge to wisdom, from efficiency to beauty, and from division to wholeness." One educational system sharing such vision is Waldorf education (McDermott, 1992). In 1919, Rudolf Steiner established the first Waldorf school in Germany (Nicholson, 2000), based on principles of Anthroposophy (Miller). Presently, there are more than 750 Waldorf schools worldwide (Nicholson, 2000). As of 2007, there were more than 30 Waldorf-inspired public schools or public schools integrating Waldorf methods in the U.S (Oberman, 2008). Public Waldorf schools "must follow the requirements of public schools, including the administration of standardized tests" (Larrison et al., 2012).

4.1 Anthroposophy

Rudolf Steiner, an Austrian philosopher and mystic (Miller), published more than 50 books and gave about 6000 lectures on topics such as science, art, education and philosophy. He is the founder of Anthroposophy (de Souza, 2012), the "philosophical foundation of Waldorf education" (Nicholson, 2000), defined by him as "'the wisdom of the human being' and as a 'path of knowledge to guide the Spiritual in the human being to the Spiritual in the universe'" (de Souza, 2012). Anthroposophy emphasizes on the "spiritual essence of the human being" (Nicholson, 2000) and "can...provide a perpetual source of knowledge and a practical method of self-development" (Nordlund, 2006). Each child transitions from the heavenly realm into the earthly realm with "intentions and latent capacities that have been developed through experiences in the spiritual world and in previous earthly lives...they carry tasks into life related to personal destiny and the goals of human evolution" (Lamb, 2012). Every human being is reincarnated on Earth to undergo particular experiences, which will contribute to the betterment of humanity and the spiritual connection between individuals (Nordlund, 2006). Each human being is "born with a unique inner self...capable of evolving toward freedom, responsibility, and maturity if appropriate nourishment and stimulation are provided at each developmental stage" (Easton, 1997).

According to the Steiner approach to education, the foundation for spiritual and individual freedom is established from the beginning of a child's life until the age of 21. "This freedom arises, not out of a declaration of the rights of the child, but out of the teacher as an authority figure undertaking the sacred task of guiding the child's spirit on its journey... authority is to be understood as part of a loving respect for the child's own being." Admiration, love and devotion for the teacher are to be innately experienced by the child rather forced upon him or her by "rules and laws of the school," which has "no value for the development of the human being." Devotion is most likely to occur when children are educated "in accordance with their own being." Through imitation of the teacher's good actions, during the early stages of their development, Waldorf students "develop security through fundamentally learning that the world is good...book learning would be regarded as out of touch with the child's nature" (Ashley, 2008).

Anthroposophy views the individual as a three-fold being (i.e., soul; spirit; body) passing through three stages of development from childhood to adulthood (Nicholson, 2000) and composed of four bodies. The physical body is "enlivened by an *etheric body* or life force." The astral body is "the individual soul in which we experience each given life." Finally, the fourth body is composed of "more universal spiritual forces that endure over our many lifetimes." The four bodies "help to create and penetrate, in particular ways, our three-fold organization" (i.e., willing; feeling; thinking). Willing is mostly concentrated in the limbs and metabolism, feeling – in the chest and thinking – in the head.

According to Steiner, "child development is an *awakening* process." The etheric body is "in the forefront" during the initial stage of child development, characterized by physical growth and "casting out old matter" (i.e., through rashes; fever) so that "it can be wholly remade." The falling of the milk teeth signals the "final thrusting out of old, inherited physical material, so that at about seven years the child's body is completely his or her own." The falling of the milk teeth also marks the time when the etheric body emerges from within the physical body where, prior to that, it had been mainly "promoting physical growth." The will must be awakened from birth to 7 years of age followed by the feelings or "*heart*" during the second developmental stage and culminating in thinking or the "*head*." Children are initially interested in the world of "*morality* or *goodness*" (i.e., imitating what is good), followed by "*beauty*" (i.e., imagination) and finally, "*truth*" (i.e., judgment). These interests are not "mutually exclusive," yet they are "in the forefront...for educating" during "certain times" (Sobo, 2012).

The "I" or individuality emanates through the willing, feeling and thinking. It is most profoundly birthed at the age of 21 when young adults "are ready to take on much more inner responsibility for their own life's direction." The "I" is strong when the will, feeling and thought have been developed in a healthy manner. The human being is now capable of higher forms of thinking and "tremendous possibilities for growth and development throughout a whole life" such as gaining "knowledge of higher worlds." Young adults would need to "work extra hard" to heal a compromised "I" so that it can "sound forth in a clear and wholesome way" (Almon).

4.2 Premises

Steiner education "promotes a non-materialistic worldview centered on the inner development of the individual and on the quality of his/her relationships with other people and with the natural environment. It also promotes a balance between the intellectual, physical, emotional, social, spiritual, and aesthetic aspects of human development" (de Souza, 2012).

***

Waldorf education is "based on the assumption that we are spiritual beings in search of development. Education should therefore help us become more human than we already are" (de Souza, 2012). The Steiner approach turns "away from war and violence toward peace and reconstruction" and is "built on coherent visions of how to improve human society by helping children realize their full potential as intelligent, creative, whole persons" (Edwards, 2002). Waldorf education is hence designed to develop the child as a whole, to foster "reinvention of human values to reincorporate the sacred" or the spiritual, recognizing "the interconnectedness of all things as a way of knowing" (Gidley, 2010).

The aim of Waldorf education is to facilitate the "life-long task of self-education" in youth (Lamb, 2012). "The ultimate goal...is freedom and autonomy" on an individual level (Ashley, 2008), the development of "free human beings who are able of themselves to impart purpose and direction to their lives" where freedom is defined as "self-knowledge, authenticity, and self-control." Such qualities are essential "if we are not to be deceived and mislead by the materialistic values and artificial needs imposed on us by the mainstream culture." Will power and self-control allow us to undertake actions towards achieving our goals and living in accordance to our values, "and not be swept away by the demands of the hegemonic forces of mainstream culture." As conceived by Steiner, freedom also signifies "our ability to intervene between stimulus and response so that we will not simply keep responding automatically to situations in which we find ourselves" (de Souza, 2012). In other words, the goal of Waldorf education is to foster holistic thinking and greater understanding of reality based on knowledge acquired through feeling, thinking, doing, consideration of truth, beauty and goodness (Easton, 1997).

Within the context of education, in 1922, Rudolf Steiner elaborated on qualities necessary to be cultivated to prepare the youth for the future: "Pedagogy…is not merely a technical art…only those who find education within the realm of morality, within the sphere of ethics, discovers it in the right way" (Gidley, 2010). "Rudolf Steiner believed in a unity of spirit, soul, and body, and that good education restores the balance between thinking, willing, and feeling" (Edwards, 2002). "In the Waldorf world view, movement or mobility also must infuse thinking and feeling for children to reach their full developmental potential. This triadic model (thought-feeling-action) stands in contrast to the dualist (mind body) model that infuses mainstream Western approaches to education" (Sobo, 2012).

In further contrast to mainstream education, the Steiner approach to education focuses on the imagination, inner development and life, rigor, awe, inquiry, aesthetics, scientific truths and models of the world (McDermott, 1992). Central to Waldorf education is "encouragement of balanced growth towards 'physical, behavioural, emotional, cognitive, social and spiritual maturation'" (Woods et al., 2005). "Love, life, wisdom and the human voice - are *central* to Steiner education but, in mainstream education, may seem *peripheral* to the '*real* task' of information acquisition" (Gidley, 2007).

Academic achievement is not the primary goal of Waldorf education and Waldorf schools do not adhere to a competitive mode of education. They are organized in a way that allows all children to "develop as healthy and responsible persons." In other words, in contrast to mainstream education, Waldorf education focuses on each child's whole being and life and not on "relative academic success...sorting and stratification." Each school day concludes with a focus on the "good points of each child" and not on his or her weaknesses. Contrary to public schools struggling with students' lack of self-esteem, through a focus on unity, responsibility and individual characteristics, Waldorf classrooms ensure that each child embodies self-esteem. Waldorf educators "have been trained to find strengths where teachers from other schools have been trained to find only weakness." While "it is as if the whole culture has conspired to throw a smokescreen around poor and minority children that conceals strengths and magnifies weaknesses," Waldorf schools are designed to accomplish the opposite in all children, indifferently of ethnicity and social class. "Waldorf education focuses immediately on what is workable for each child." Finally, Waldorf education is structured in a way that minimizes unneeded hierarchy. Waldorf schools are directed by Waldorf educators and not by a formal administration. Waldorf teachers receive a wage that reflects "current efforts rather than mere seniority" (McDermott, 1992).

4.3 Curriculum

"It is only when we, as educators, look deeply within ourselves and strive to embody wholeness in our own lives, that we will inspire our students to do the same. Our lives make up the curriculum" (Miller, 2001). "Steiner himself stressed on many occasions that the 'curriculum' was not a fixed abstract thing but needs to be created from moment to moment" (Gidley, 2007).

***

Waldorf schools teach the academic disciplines offered through most of mainstream education (de Souza, 2012), namely, all National Curriculum subjects (Ashley). There are no exams, tests or failing grades as part of Waldorf education (Ribeiro & de Jesus Pereira, 2007). The Steiner approach values the partnership with parents (Edwards, 2002). Research demonstrates that "the greater the family and community involvement in schools, the greater the students' achievement" (Leu, 2008).

The Waldorf curriculum is "organized in an 'ascending spiral' approach" (i.e., "many of the main themes of the curriculum are repeated at varying degrees of depth and complexity at subsequent grade levels"). Repetition and a deliberate sense of rhythmic pattern are part of the curriculum and of the daily classroom routine in a Waldorf school (Nicholson, 2000). One purpose of the rhythmic or patterned nature of the curriculum is to ensure that children know what to expect of the school day. Lack of such awareness leads to "tension…nervousness" and therefore "ill health" such as "unhealthful inner 'contractions' in their organs" (Sobo, 2012).

Daily instruction in Waldorf schools revolves around the "main lesson," a 2-hour lesson, part of the "lesson block" or main lesson unit (Nicholson, 2000), taught daily over a period of 3-4 weeks (Ribeiro & de Jesus Pereira, 2007). The 2-hour main lesson blocks allow students to study a subject in depth without interruptions (de Souza, 2012). Primary sources are the preferred reference point while textbook use is "generally discouraged." Each student has a "main lesson book," serving as "both text and assessment portfolio" (Nicholson, 2000). The emotional/organic connection to the new subject precedes the intellectual engagement with the subject (de Souza, 2012). In other words, an "intense experience" of science subjects is followed by intellectual conceptualization (Ribeiro & de Jesus Pereira, 2007). Waldorf teachers posit that "a precocious focus on intellectual development impairs the healthy and balanced development of children's emotional, physical, social, aesthetic, and spiritual natures" (de Souza, 2012). Thinking, feeling and willing are both "distinct" as well as growing phases during the entire course of Waldorf education. "The claim would be that a thinking teenager remains a feeling one. This is reflected in the Waldorf curriculum itself" (Ashley, 2008).

"At Waldorf or Steiner schools...an integrative approach prevails" (Sobo, 2012). The lesson block "incorporates multiple forms of representation around a principal theme." Oral presentation is the primary means through which the teacher relates information. He or she engages in asking students questions and involving them in discussion and daily reviews, creating "a sort of 'Socratic dialogue'" between the teacher and his or her students (Nicholson, 2000). Cultivating the imagination through mediums such as story-telling and creative arts, is designed to facilitate students' ability to "envision prospective futures, which are different from the present" (Gidley, 2010).

Arts do not represent a separate subject, but are rather integrated within the Waldorf curriculum from 1st through 8th grade. Each subject during this period "is taught in an artistic way" (Ribeiro & de Jesus Pereira, 2007). Artistic form is embedded within the Waldorf curriculum for purposes of expanding and deepening the "intellectual experiences of the students, stimulating the senses, enriching the imagination, and cultivating feeling" (Nicholson, 2000). Creative arts in Waldorf schools are taught as they "allow a child to experience a subject on a far deeper, richer level than the intellectual one...Information can be gathered or retrieved, but the experience of the subjects through individual work and through the arts builds a foundation in the soul that will enrich all further learning and the whole of a student's life" (de Souza, 2012). Singing and reciting in unison organized around the theme of the lesson block aim to foster moral responsibility, unity and cooperation (Nicholson, 2000).

In regards to nature, the Waldorf curriculum aims at cultivating the theme of conservation or "how man works through nature to make the world a fit place for human habitation" through activities such as building (i.e., hen house) and study of minerals (Ashley, 2008). The outdoors is common for teaching the Waldorf curriculum (de Souza, 2012).

There is a misconception that since anthroposophy is mainly based on esoteric science, Waldorf schools portray "a strange religious cult." Waldorf school students do not receive instruction in anthroposophy; anthroposophical principles simply "govern the pedagogy." (Ashley, 2008). Three ways Waldorf education fosters spiritual development is through encouraging mindfulness, achievement to the highest potential in every undertaking and revering "everything that generates and gives meaning to life" such as "mother nature" (de Souza, 2012).

Waldorf teachers remain with the same class from 1st to 8th grade to ensure that "an intimate, stable, and continuous relationship with a mentor" is established. Such relationship "cannot be achieved when there is a change of teacher from year to year." Lack of connection between teacher and student and the possibility that a teacher cannot master the educational material for 8 grades are drawbacks to such an approach. Some Waldorf schools have addressed the latter weakness by inviting academic discipline-specific specialist teachers to build on the knowledge introduced by the class teacher (de Souza, 2012). Students remain in the same group from the 1st through the 12th grades (Ribeiro & de Jesus Pereira, 2007).

Waldorf teachers express concerns regarding the influence of electronic mediums such as the Internet and television in children's development and learning considering "the extent to which the media have been affecting our values, habits, lifestyles, and the way that we relate with the world and people around us." The Waldorf curriculum "protects children's right to be children and not have to worry about certain problems and responsibilities while they are still young." According to Waldorf educators, students "will have plenty of time to engage with these kinds of problems outside school" (de Souza, 2012).

4.3.1 0-21

Learning in Waldorf schools takes place "in a developmentally appropriate way" (Sobo, 2012). Students' developmental stage guides the content of the subject being taught (Ribeiro & de Jesus Pereira, 2007).

4.3.1.1 0-7

Early childhood or the first developmental stage of "imitation" and "will" lasts until approximately age 7 (Nicholson, 2000). Children are still "coming down" from the "spiritual" or heavenly realm during their first stage of development. Therefore, a major task of the teacher as elaborated by a Waldorf educator is to "help them come down" (Sobo, 2012).

The Waldorf kindergarten focuses on nurturing seven primary skills in children up to the age of 6 or 7. These include: body and movement, imagination and creativity, speech, senses and perception, concentration and motivation, social ability, moral values and ethics. According to researchers, more than 50% of first-grade students experience weight, balance and posture problems. The large and fine motor skills of a number of children are not fully developed and they "suffer from lack of movement." Since a person's spiritual and mental balance are associated with his or her physical mobility, lack of physical balance translates into mental imbalance. Speech acquisition is further associated with a person's ability for physical mobility. This is the reason the Waldorf curriculum incorporates physical movement in the form of activities such as games, handwork, gardening and walks (Lang, 2003).

Learning in Waldorf schools prior to age 7 takes place through imitation and play (i.e., cultivating the will or learning to control body movement and the limbs) (Woods et al., 2005). Children, according to the Steiner approach, "learn, in great part, through imitation." From that perspective, it is not sufficient for teachers to instruct children verbally. "If we are to really educate children, we need to start by educating ourselves. It is what we do, and not necessarily what we tell children to do, that will effectively influence them" (de Souza, 2012).

"Today many children, youth, and adults suffer from nervousness, hyperactivity, and a lack of concentration." Waldorf kindergarten educators present to students "interesting and stimulating possibilities for activity" which "have a motivating effect on the children" (Lang, 2003). Imaginary play is central to the Waldorf kindergarten curriculum as it allows for emotional, intellectual and physical growth (Edwards, 2002). Making "'barely finished' toys" available to Waldorf kindergarten students stimulates and develops students' creativity and imagination (Lang, 2003). Oral ("never written") language, song, story, bodily exploration, creative and constructive play also take a prominent place in the Waldorf kindergarten curriculum. Through such activities, children develop motivation and the ability to concentrate (Edwards, 2002). According to Steiner's approach to education, it is vital to cultivate children's will during their first years of life. Failing to nourish the child's will or enabling the child to accomplish what he or she needs and wants with dedication and care at an early age would likely lead to the child becoming "undisciplined and slovenly" as he or she grows older. A disciplined will is also important for the development of strength the child needs to meet his or her goals later in life (de Souza, 2012).

"School readiness should be determined by the actual physical and mental development of the child, and this is not necessarily in step with legal regulations or economic considerations...Quite the opposite is true! The time before school, free from formal learning, allows for the development of basic skills on which later formal education and training can build." The Waldorf kindergarten exemplifies such notion. It is "intended to better the developmental conditions of each child and afford him or her a happy and learning-intensive childhood" (Lang, 2003).

Nowadays, the great majority of schools begin to teach children reading, writing and math as early as preschool. According to Waldorf educators, the foundation for healthy emotions, physical and social development is established during the first years of life. Such foundation may not be established if children are mostly occupied with writing, reading and studying (de Souza, 2012). In contrast to public education, the Steiner approach to education delays the introduction of reading and math. Research findings demonstrate the "push for early academics" as exemplified by mainstream education "can have negative consequences." Stressing "on early academics may draw brain resources that are needed for the maximal functionality and neural connectivity of sensory and motor systems." Additional research indicates that "early academics do not relate to improved academic performance in later years and, to the contrary, appear to relate to poorer relational skills and life outcome" (Larrison & Daly, 2011). Formal instruction in

Waldorf pre-K and kindergarten "would cause premature hardening of the intellect, leading to inflexible thinking in adulthood" (Sobo, 2012). Formal learning begins at age 7 (Woods et al., 2005). Reading is not taught until 1st grade (Nicholson, 2000).

4.3.1.2 7-14

Middle childhood takes place between the ages of 7 and 14. Imagination, feelings and experience are "the strongest factors in learning" during this stage of developmental. Middle childhood story-telling or the process of "discovering and sharing...moral truths" is "at the heart of a Waldorf lesson, regardless of the subject area." It engages students' feelings and experience and exemplifies the teacher as a "transmitter of truths...consistent, guiding authority, trusted and respected by the students." Lessons during middle childhood, and especially during the early grades, are organized around legends, mythology, folk tales, pictures and parables which evoke the imagination and the feeling pertinent to this stage of development. A sixth-grade Waldorf teacher would therefore teach mediaeval history through developmentally-appropriate means such as creative writing, music, story-telling, singing and group-recitation (Nicholson, 2000). The emotional connection established with the subject being learned allows children to "feel motivated to learn and to make sense of what they are learning." The imagination is critically important as it not only "intensifies our feeling life and it is through it that we can visualize new and better possibilities for our lives and for solving our problems," but it also allows for the experience of a deeper understanding of the world (de Souza, 2012). Through activities such as story-telling, the 7-14 Waldorf curriculum is sequenced and structured without the use of textbooks. Such approach to education focuses on students' memory and oral listening abilities. Children compose their own lesson books based on what they have learned, preserving it "in their own personal format, documents and treasures of their learning experiences" (Edwards, 2002).

Between 7 and 14, Waldorf students' "sense of value" is nurtured through feelings, withdrawn from a variety of artistic approaches. Feelings allow children to perceive the world as beautiful, "to develop intimate and lasting connections with those structures, beings and representations that make it so. The child is not yet ready to confront the ugliness and brutality that is environmental degradation and inhumanity" (Ashley, 2008). The middle childhood stage is mainly a "teacher-directed phase" as students at this stage "have a need for adult direction and supervision, though not a dictatorial style of enforcement." The teacher exemplifies a "loving authority."

Reading is gradually introduced in 1st grade (Nicholson, 2000) through a method compatible with children's developmental stage (Ogletree, 1975). The order of reading instruction is as following: oral language experience to written language and finally reading (Schmitt-Stegmann, 1997) while the goal of reading instruction is to integrate intellectual development with artistic creativity and practical skills through engaging the feelings. The approach of teaching reading is more gradual and multi-sensory compared to public schools with the focus of instruction grounded in engaging children in a variety of artistic activities to foster learning (Ward, 2003).

4.3.1.3 14-21

Adolescence and young adulthood from age 14 on, mark the last stage in human development. It is the stage of the "intellect," characterized by emerging sense of independence and intellectual thought (Nicholson, 2000).

In contrast to mainstream education, Waldorf schools do not espouse "early closure," "citizen science" or the introduction and immersion of children as young as the preschool level in social and environmental issues (i.e., nuclear power; sustainable development). According to Steiner's approach to education, "debating stem cell research or nuclear power is not believed to be suitable activity for the under 16s." From the age of 14 onwards, students begin to generate new questions and meaning in regards to prior impressions and feelings. The primary learning task is to allow students to reach to their own scientific conclusions such as that the "world is threatened," not to teach that it is (Ashley, 2008).

4.4 Studies

"The empirical research on Waldorf education is surprisingly limited given its nearly 100 year history" (Larrison et al., 2012). Yet, "there is a growing body of research substantiating Waldorf practices and curriculum and their holistic, balanced approach to education" (Syringa Mountain School, 2013).

Case-studies on 22 Waldorf schools demonstrated that Waldorf education "offers alternatives to a number of deeply embedded structural or ideological constraints" such as: a) economic prosperity and individualism as positive and "an end in itself;" b) youth regarded as "future units of economic production" rather than as spiritual beings seeking fulfilment; c) the child's spirit and child development ceasing to guide the curriculum; d) students' inability to "obtain a sense of higher meaning or purpose" due to the fragmented nature of the academic curriculum; e) "frequently fragmented and discontinuous" experience of mentoring; f) "science education in disarray" and often rejected by students; g) humanities and arts perceived as "frivolous in comparison to subjects associated with economic utility" (Ashley, 2008).

4.4.1 Academic, Cognitive and Social Skills

Studies on private as well as public Waldorf schools demonstrate "a positive impact of Waldorf on academic achievement" (Larrison et al., 2012).

***

A recent study compared the 2-year academic performance of national and California Waldorf students to mainstream education students. Findings revealed lower reading and math scores for Waldorf students in the early grades, yet significantly higher scores by the 7th and 8th grades, hence a gradual increase in reading and math performance (Larrison & Daly, 2011). A 2011 study compared the standardized test scores in math and reading of public Waldorf and public schools. Results showed that the test scores of Waldorf students were lower than the test scores of public school students in kindergarten and the early grades, "followed by higher levels of advanced performance by the 8th grade." A 2009 study conducted in New Zealand demonstrated that Waldorf students who had not received formal reading instruction in pre-school or kindergarten lagged behind in reading ability by the age of 10, yet no difference in reading scores was evident in reading achievement between students who had received reading instruction in pre-school or kindergarten and students who had not at around age 10. Similarly, a 2008 study revealed that students from 4 public schools using Waldorf methods in California performed poorer on math and language arts in the 2nd grade compared to their traditional public school peers, yet either matched or performed better than their public school peers by the 8th grade. The researcher of the study, Ida Oberman, "concluded that the Waldorf approach successfully laid the groundwork for future academics by first engaging students through integrated arts lessons and strong relationships instead of preparing them for standardized tests" (Syringa Mountain School, 2013).

A study conducted by Schieffer and Busse (2001) compared national assessment performance scores of 4th-grade students in the Urban Waldorf School and a public neighboring school with demographics similar to the Urban Waldorf School. Overall, Waldorf school students scored higher on standardized tests compared to public school students (Larrison et al., 2012).

The Thomas E. Mathews Community School in California "serves high-risk juvenile offenders, many of whom have learning disabilities." The school transitioned to Waldorf methods in the 1990s. A study conducted in 1999 demonstrated that students exhibited "improved attitudes toward learning, better social interaction and excellent academic progress… The study also found significant improvements in reading and math scores, student participation, focus, openness and enthusiasm, as well as emotional stability, civility of interaction and tenacity."

A different study revealed that the SAT scores of Waldorf students exceeded the national average, particularly on verbal measures while another study showed that Waldorf graduates passed the college-entrance exams in Germany at "double to triple the rate of students graduating from the state education system." Research conducted in 2006 showed that Austrian Waldorf students "are above average in science" (Syringa Mountain School, 2013).

Last, but not least, the available research on Waldorf education suggests a "positive impact of Waldorf on a number of cognitive and social outcome measures." It is correlated with greater critical thinking skills, social skills, creativity and "engagement as global citizens." Waldorf students have been found to exhibit "more mature social and moral impulses," including "a reduction in bullying of peers" (Larrison et al., 2012).

4.4.2 Creativity

A recent study comparing the drawing performance of Waldorf, Montessori and traditional schools showed that "the approach to art education in Steiner schools is conducive not only to more highly rated imaginative drawings in terms of general drawing ability and use of color but also to more accurate and detailed observational drawings." Yet another study revealed that, on average, Waldorf students performed better on the Torrance Test of Creative Thinking Ability compared to their state-school peers (Syringa Mountain School, 2013).

4.4.3 Vision of Future

A qualitative study examined the vision of 128 senior Waldorf secondary students in Australia held for the future. In contrast to mainstream students who envisioned techno-fix solutions for the future, Steiner students stressed on humanness or social-based solutions (i.e., activism; changes in values; spirituality expressed through consciousness development; personal and community empowerment; education for future care; interconnectedness; social diversity; equality; tolerance and community; "a peaceful, communicative world;" "re-sacralising of nature and humanity"). As also contrasted to many mainstream students, Steiner students "were not disempowered by...negative future expectations, but rather, demonstrated a strong sense of activism to create more positive futures." They have embodied "very richly imaginative positive visions of their preferred futures" (Gidley, 2010).

4.4.4 Waldorf Graduates

1,124 Waldorf graduates (30-37, 50-59 and 62-66 years of age) completed qualitative interviews and written surveys. Former Waldorf students "do not tend towards institutional forms of religion" and they were able to "develop their own 'spiritual path.'" 87% of Waldorf graduates "felt a sense of belonging" to their school while 80% "have felt very well [comfortable] there." The majority of the participants would attend Waldorf school again while 47% of those who had children enrolled their children in a Waldorf school. Not being able to afford Waldorf schooling, Waldorf school not in proximity to residence and alternative approaches also suggested as effective, were the reasons the remaining Waldorf graduate parents chose not to enroll their children in a Waldorf school. Waldorf graduates reflected on the Waldorf curriculum as "interested…diversified…meaningful." The the relationship between teachers and students was evaluated as positive. Waldorf graduates viewed Waldorf schools as favorably influencing the development of social skills (i.e., empathy; cooperation; consideration), personality (i.e., creativity; flexibility; sense of worth; self-assurance) as well as self-reliance and the ability to form personal opinion (Mitchell & Gerwin, 2007).

527 graduates (1943-2005) from 27 Waldorf schools participated in the Survey of Waldorf Graduates, Phase II. Findings revealed that Waldorf education is achieving: a) "thinkers who think outside the box;" b) "high levels of social intelligence;" c) "basis for moral navigation;" d) "creative problem solving;" e) "environmental stewardship;" f) "high levels of emotional intelligence;" g) "global consciousness and sustainability," and h) "multiple intelligences and cross disciplinary learners." Three main findings were identified. First, Waldorf graduates are able to "think for themselves" and translate their ideas into practice. They value and engage in "life-long learning" and possess a "highly developed sense for aesthetics." Second, Waldorf graduates "value lasting human relationships – and they seek out

opportunities to be of help to other people." Third, the personal and professional lives of Waldorf graduates are guided by an "inner moral compass." They exercise "high ethical principles into their chosen professions" (Survey of Waldorf graduates).

A study conducted by the Education Department of Bonn, Germany, and published in 1981, included a sample of 460 Waldorf graduates born between 1946 and 1947. Results showed that Waldorf graduates performed three times better on Abitur tests compared to students from State schools. The U.S. tests equivalent to the Abitur tests would permit students to begin college directly from the sophomore level. Results from this study further demonstrated that 20% of Waldorf graduates chose to be employed in the social and educational fields, 12% - in the artistic/linguistic area and 12% - in the medical field. Only a very small percentage chose to work in the legal and technical areas. Waldorf graduates "tended not to show an interest in success, prestige, recognition or financial concerns when choosing their professions" (de Souza, 2012).

Discussion

Waldorf education rejects disparaging educational practices (i.e., focus on materialism; technology; efficiency; intellect; academic achievement; limited, non-contextual knowledge acquisition; physical immobility; linear development/intelligence; negative emotional and thought states; exams; grades; rewards and punishments) pertinent to mainstream education while closely reflecting research and professional recommendations in regards to children's optimal growth, development and educational practices (i.e., focus on spiritual development through nurturing the innate unfoldment of lifelong learning; authenticity; freedom; autonomy; unfoldment of personal potential; cultivation of wisdom, high consciousness values, imagination, creativity, positive thoughts and emotions, physical well-being, expression of inner self; no exams, grades, rewards or punishments).

The difference in instructional approaches between mainstream and Waldorf education is further reflected in the outcomes associated with either method. While mainstream students feel "disempowered by… negative future expectations" and "envisioned techno-fix," virtual or transhumanist "solutions for the future," Waldorf education students "stressed on humanness or social-based solutions…embodied 'very richly imaginative positive visions of their preferred futures'" and "demonstrated a strong sense of activism to create more positive futures." Mainstream students' vision results in "the concentration of profit and power in the hands of corporations" and the subsequent "deterioration of earth" (*Earth, 2.31*) while Waldorf students' vision culminates in "the realization that Earth is a living being and we are part of nature, dependent on the environment for our survival…challenging us to live in an ecologically sound way and to develop an approach to education that cultivates the heart as well as the mind, inspires cooperation rather than competition, empathy and love instead of violence and hate" (*Earth, 2.31*). Waldorf education is therefore a preferable alternative to mainstream education.

Yet, "Steiner himself stressed on many occasions that the 'curriculum' was not a fixed abstract thing but needs to be created from moment to moment." It is therefore imperative that the corporate profit-based knowledge that educators at Waldorf schools choose to impart (i.e., teaching National Curriculum subjects) is reconsidered in light of the "great diversity of developmental trajectories" (*Development, 2.8*) and each student's "unique inner self…capable of evolving toward freedom, responsibility… maturity" and "developing to…maximum personal potential" (*Spirituality, 1.2*).

Last, but not least, Rudolf Steiner developed the premises of Waldorf education or "the right kind of education" (*Reward and Punishment, 2.18*) prior to 1919 or before the emergence of sound research confirming the validity and reliability of his theory, anthroposophy. The only meaningful explanation applicable to such finding is embedded within the fact that his consciousness or spiritual sense awareness had expanded beyond the limits of the "common brain patterns" (*Mainstream Education*); Rudolph Steiner had gained access to the "'path of knowledge to guide the Spiritual in the human being to the Spiritual in the universe.'" Such finding further confirms the innate nature of spirituality and its importance in the evolution of consciousness and life.

References

Almon, J. Educating for creative thinking: The Waldorf approach.

Ashley, M. (2008). Here's what you must think about nuclear power: Grappling with the spiritual ground of children's judgement inside and outside Steiner Waldorf education. *International Journal of Children's Spirituality, 13*(1), 65-74.

de Souza, D. L. (2012). Learning and human development in Waldorf pedagogy and curriculum. *ENCOUNTER: Education for Meaning and Social Justice, 25*(4), 50-62.

Easton, F. (1997). Educating the whole child, "Head, Heart, and Hands": Learning from the Waldorf experience. *Theory into Practice, 36*(2), 87-94.

Edwards, C. P. (2002). Three approaches from Europe: Waldorf, Montessori, and Reggio Emilia. 1-16. *Early Childhood Research & Practice, 4*(1), 1-16.

Gidley, J. M. (2010). Holistic education and visions of rehumanized futures. *Research on Steiner Education, 1*(2), 139-147.

Lang, P. (2003). The kindergarten child. *Association of Waldorf Schools of North America*, 13-16.

Lamb, G. (2012). The social mission of Waldorf education. *Association of Waldorf Schools of North America*, 1-131.

Leu, J. C.-Y. (2008). Early childhood music education in Taiwan: An ecological systems perspective. *Arts Education Policy Review, 109*(3), 17-26.

Larrison, A. L. & Daly, A. J. (2011). Holistic education and the brain: A look at Steiner-Waldorf education. 1-27.

Larrison, A. L., Daly, A. J. & VanVooren, C. (2012). Twenty years and counting: A look at Waldorf in the public sector using online sources. *Current Issues in Education, 15*(3), 1-24.

McDermott, R. (1992). Waldorf education in America: A promise and its problems. *ReVision, 15*(2), 1-14.

Miller, R. A brief history of alternative education. Retrieved from http://southerncrossreview.org/55/miller-education.htm

Miller, R. (2001). Making connections to the world some thoughts on holistic curriculum. *ENCOUNTER: Education for Meaning and Social Justice, 14*(4), 29-35.

Mitchell, D. & Gerwin, D. (2007). Alumni of German and Swiss Waldorf schools – An empiric study on education and creative living. *Research Institute for Waldorf Education*, 1-4.

Nicholson, D. W. (2000). Layers of experience: Forms of representation in a Waldorf school classroom. *Journal of Curriculum Studies, 32(4)*, 575-587.

Nordlund, C. Y. (2006). Art experiences in Waldorf education: Graduates' meaning making reflections. 1-238.

Oberman, I. (2008). Waldorf education and its spread into the public sector research findings. *ENCOUNTER: Education for Meaning and Social Justice, 21*(2), 10-14.

Ogletree, E. J. (1975). Geometric form drawing: A perceptual-motor approach to preventive remediation (The Steiner approach). *Journal of Special Education,9*(3), 237-245.

Ribeiro, W. & de Jesus Pereira, J. P. (2007). Seven "myths" about the social participation of Waldorf graduates. *The Online Waldorf Library*, *15*(2), 1-17.

Schmitt-Stegmann, A. (1997). Child development and curriculum in Waldorf Education. *Reports-Descriptive*, 1-15.

Sobo, E. (2012). "This is Not Head-to-Head Education": Whole child development in a Waldorf school. *Learning In and Out of School: Education across the Globe*, 1-25.

Survey of Waldorf graduates: Phase II. *Research Institute for Waldorf Education*, 1-55.

Syringa Mountain School (2013). Syringa Mountain School: Cultivating the head, heart and hands. 1-122.

Ward, W. (2003). Learning to read & write in the Waldorf schools. *Journal for Waldorf/Rudolf Steiner Teachers*, *8*(2).

Woods, P., Ashley, M. & Woods, G. (2005). Steiner schools in England. *Research Report*, *645*, 1-206.

Chapter 5

AUTISM AND VACCINATION

5.1. Autism

Pervasive developmental disorders (PDD) is the equivalent name for autism spectrum disorders (ASD) (Meilleur & Fombonne, 2009). ASD is a "neurodevelopmental syndrome with onset before the age of 36 months" (Yassa, 2014). Autism, Asperger syndrome, childhood disintegrative disorder, Rett syndrome and pervasive developmental disorder fall under the category of ASD (Savoy, 2014). Research findings demonstrated that "the development of infants later diagnosed with ASD differs already from that of their typical peers during the period from 2 to 6 months of age" (Jones & Klin, 2013). ASD is characterized by social skills deficits, repetitive and limited interests and behaviors (O'Dwyer et al., 2014), communication impairments (Savoy, 2014) and motor deficits (Markoulakis et al., 2012). ASDs affect about 1 in 88 individuals (Jones & Klin, 2013).

Recent studies found an increase in the incidence of autism from 1 in 2,500 children in mid-1980s to 1 in 300 children in 1996 and thus "confirmed that the rise in the prevalence in autism reflects genuine phenomena and is not the result of population migration, differences in autism diagnoses or other potential confounders" (Geier & Geier, 2003). Centers for Disease Control and Prevention's (CDC) Autism and Developmental Disabilities Monitoring (ADDM) Network reported a 78% increase in the prevalence of ASD between 2002 and 2008 (Yassa, 2014).

Based on estimates established by the CDC, 560,000 people in the U.S. are diagnosed with autism (Moreland, 2008). According to CDC and the National Health Interview Survey (NHIS), the prevalence of ASD as reported by parents has increased 4 times between 1997-1999 and 2006-2008 (Yassa, 2014). The CDC further reported a 57% increase in prevalence of ASD among 8-year old children in 10 U.S. sites (Pinborough-Zimmerman et al., 2012).

96% of children with ASD also have a comorbid developmental disability such as learning disability (i.e., 60%), ADHD (i.e., 42%) and generalized developmental delay (i.e., 80%) (Savoy, 2014). Between 50% and 83% of autistic children meet the diagnostic threshold for ADHD (Clarke et al., 2011). Less than 19% of children with ASD have an intellectual disability (Savoy, 2014).

Data collected by the U.S. Department of Education reveals a 528% increase (i.e., from 15,580 to 97,904) of students with autism from 1992-1993 to 2001-2002 and an increase from 3.64 to 20.53 public school enrollees with autism during the same time period (Safran, 2008). The number of children with ASD in special education has "nearly doubled from 2.3% in the 2002-2003 school year to 4.4% in 2007-2008" (Pinborough-Zimmerman et al., 2012).

"The decision to screen all children remains a controversial one." Redundant testing, "overdiagnosis due to false positives associated with traditional screening methods" and anxiety are some of the reasons cited by opponents of universal ASD screening (Savoy, 2014).

5.1.1 Genetic and Environmental Factors

"The cause of autism remains vague." Genetic, environmental and immunological factors as well as greater susceptibility to oxidative stress are all considered to influence the development of autism (Yassa, 2014). Environmental and genetic factors have the potential to "disrupt" the normal development of the nervous system, "interfering" with the formation, migration and connection of neurons as well as the formation of synapses, "ultimately causing autism" (Kalkbrenner et al., 2014). A multitude rather than a single gene has been suggested to influence autism (Yassa, 2014).

The National Research Council (NRC) reported that 28% of developmental disabilities have their origins in environmental factors (Trasande, 2014). The past decade was marked by an exponential increase in the number of epidemiological studies examining the association between exposure to environmental chemicals and autism. Environmental chemicals may specifically disrupt the nervous system's cells and structure, impact the immune and endocrine systems, contribute to epigenetic changes, "and more." The impact of environmental chemicals on such processes has been supported by data while the topic has received growing attention. "It is now understood that environmental factors play a larger role in causing autism than previously thought...Out of a chemical universe topping 80,000 agents, over 1000 have laboratory evidence of neurotoxicity, but only a small fraction have been studied in humans during critical windows of development. Human exposures to these chemicals are common" (Kalkbrenner et al., 2014).

Postulated to influence autism environmental agents include lead, mercury, measles, retinoic acid, maternal thalidomide, rubella virus, alcohol use during gestation and valproic acid (Yassa, 2014). "Lead and mercury have strong and consistent evidence of harming the developing nervous system" even at "typical exposure levels leading to 'silent toxicity.'" Metals cross the blood-brain barrier and the placenta, "accumulate in developing brains, and interact at the cellular level" (Kalkbrenner et al., 2014). Decreased rate of excretion of lead and mercury rather increased exposure are implied in the etiology of autism. The half-life of lead and mercury ranges between weeks and months, causing such toxic metals to leave the blood and enter tissues and or/bones, potentially causing neural impairments. Windham et al. (2006) revealed a probable connection between heavy

125

metals and autism while Blaurock-Busch et al. (2011), Blaurock-Busch et al. (2012), Lyall et al. (2014) and Rossignol et al. (2014) demonstrated that heavy metals lead to autism (Yassa, 2014).

The purposes of a recent study were to investigate the association between lead and/or mercury and autism and to test the effectiveness of chelating agents in improving symptoms of autism. Hair and blood sample from 45 Upper Egypt children with autism between 2 and 10 years of age and 45 control group children of the same age were obtained and analyzed for lead and mercury levels. Results from both test and control groups were analyzed, followed by treatment of the autistic children group with chelating, designed to detoxify the system from lead and mercury. "Lead and mercury" were "considered as one of the main causes of autism." The autistic symptoms of the autistic group treated with chelating played a "great role in improvement of those kids," specifically in the areas of unintentional movement, word and sentence formation. Adams et al. (2009 a,b) arrived at similar results. Study findings demonstrated a positive association between prenatal or early postnatal exposure to lead and/or mercury, elevated lead and/or mercury levels in children and improved autistic symptoms following chelating treatment (Yassa, 2014). A third study demonstrated that mercury contained in dental amalgam was positively correlated with increased severity of autism.

Human fetuses "can be exposed" to air pollutant chemicals (i.e., airborne metals) such as mercury and lead. A recent review summarized findings from studies examining the association between autism and exposure to air pollutants, tobacco, metals, pesticides, volatile organic compounds and organic endocrine-disrupting compounds. A positive correlation was established between autism, air pollutants, several metals and pesticides and a "suggestive trends" for some phthalates and volatile organic compounds such as styrene, trichloroethylene and methylene chloride.

More than 13% of pregnant women smoked cigarettes in the U.S. between 1999 and 2006. Direct and second-hand smoke contains "thousands of chemicals" such as volatile organic compounds, nicotine and metals (i.e., cadmium; lead). Exposure to direct and second-hand smoke "are strongly suspected to disrupt the developing nervous system."

"Over 600 unique chemical pesticides and 20,000 commercial pesticide products...are on the market, and over one billion pounds are used in the U.S. each year." Organochlorines (OC) and organophosphates (OP) are pesticide classes with greatest evidence of neurotoxicity. Study findings revealed that OC pesticides were present in more than 97% of biosamples in the U.S. while the percentage for OP pesticides accounted for 70% of biosamples. Pesticides have the capability of passing through the blood-brain barrier and the placenta. OP pesticides "inhibit acetylycholinest erase production in the brain, restricting neurotransmission in the peripheral and central nervous systems, ultimately impacting synapse formation, axon transmission, cell maturation, and programmed cell death." OC, on the other hand, "act on the nervous system via gamma aminobutyric acid (GABA) receptor-mediated chloride ion channels and may also derail neurodevelopment through their endocrine-disrupting properties." OP and OC pesticides are primarily used in agriculture and therefore diet is the main route of exposure to OC and OP pesticides. Research studies have demonstrated that some pesticides cause neurodevelopmental impairments. A secondary route of exposure include inhalation from pesticide application on agricultural fields and direct contact (i.e., dermal absorption). "OC pesticides are persistent pollutants and some are detectable in the environment and human tissues decades after they have been banned, such as the OC pesticide DDT." Exposure to pesticides coincides with exposure to other factors which may benefit (i.e., vitamins and minerals derived from grains, fruits and vegetables) or cause harm to the nervous system (Kalkbrenner et al., 2014).

The costs associated with autism attributable to environmental contaminants in 2008 in the U.S. accounted to $7.9 billion. "These large economic costs of autism attributable to environmental chemicals beg the question why they occur in the first place. Economists use the term externality to indicate when entities gain economically from activities that result in harm to others. In environmental health, exposures produced by industrial activities produce health hazards that affect lives of people who are not involved in the economic activity" (Trasande, 2014).

5.1.2 Treatment

There is no effective treatment for ASD, only "an array of potential ASD therapies" such as medication, diet and behavioral interventions. "Only a few have ample evidence of efficacy." Psychiatrist, other mental health practitioner, developmental pediatrician, neurologist, audiologist, physical therapist and special education teacher are typically involved in the "evaluation and management" of children with ASD. Part C of the 2004 Individuals with Disabilities Education Act requires that all U.S. states grant access to early intervention programs (Savoy, 2014).

5.2 Vaccination

Immunization of children in the U.S. and in a number of developed countries has "virtually eliminated" a number of diseases such as measles, tetanus and rubella (Bale, 2004).

5.2.1 Policy

"Vaccine mandates are matters of state law." The Advisory Committee on Immunization Practices of the CDC and the US Food and Drug Administration (FDA) must approve state vaccine mandates prior to their implementation (Lillvis et al., 2014). State mandates require childhood vaccination prior to school or daycare entry (Stratton et al., 2001).

A number of states grant vaccination exemption for religious, philosophical or medical reasons. When permitted, religious exemption is granted on the basis of the "free exercise clause of the First Amendment." It was found that, as of 2012, 48 states had religious exemptions, 22 states had philosophical exemptions and 50 states – medical exemptions. The religious/philosophical exemptions of 10 states were found to be unclear while the religious/philosophical exemptions of 6 states – "ambiguously worded...Most parents seeking an exemption because of vaccine safety concerns find the philosophical exemption to be the best-fitting justification." Exemption based on evidence-based immunity to disease is also granted in some states. According to findings from a recently published study, "while more bills had been introduced to broaden vaccine exemptions, only those tightening the exemption policies actually passed."

"Vaccine-critical activists have made much of the fact that vaccines contain formaldehyde or mercury, or may have been developed with cell lines originally obtained from aborted human fetuses (eg, rubella, varicella, and hepatitis A). Introducing bills requiring that parents be informed about vaccine ingredients is part of a strategy to heighten perceptions that vaccines are dangerous." In an attempt for vaccine policy change, vaccine critics further argued that "vaccines were risky" and "that the government was responsible for lax oversight of profiteering pharmaceutical companies." Yet, the "political leverage of these arguments weakened" by arguments disputing such claims (Lillvis et al., 2014).

5.2.2 Thimerosal

The FDA requires that multi-dose vials of vaccines contain preservatives that serve the purpose of preventing fungal or bacterial contamination. Thimerosal is an organic mercury compound that has been used in pharmaceuticals and vaccines as a preservative since the 1930s. Aside from its use as a preservative, thimerosal is also used as a bacteriostatic agent in vaccine manufacturing. Thimerosal consists of 49.6% mercury ("known neurotoxicant") by weight and is metabolized as thiosalicylate and ethylmercury. The whole-cell pertussis vaccine (DTP) was the sole recommended vaccine for infants containing thimerosol prior to 1991 (Stratton et al., 2001).

By 1997, vaccines including diphtheria-tetanus toxoids and pertussis as well diphtheria tetanus toxoids and acellular pertussis had contained thimerosal (Bale, 2004). By 1999, more than 30 "licenses and marketed" vaccines (including vaccines for infants) contained thimerosol (Stratton et al., 2001). In 1999, the FDA "realized...that a child could potentially be exposed to more ethyl mercury (as thimerosal) through the recommended vaccine schedule than the Environmental Protection Agency (EPA) limit for methyl mercury, which is a different type of mercury that is a known environmental contaminant in fish. Methyl mercury was well studied at the time, but ethyl mercury was not, and it did not have its own safety standard" (Lillvis et al., 2014). FDA contacted vaccine manufacturers in 1999, seeking an explanation for the "continued use" of thimerosal in vaccines and inquiring on their intentions of removing it. "A joint statement was issued in July 1999 by the American Academy of Pediatrics (AAP) and the U.S. Public Health Service (PHS) recommending removal of thimerosal from vaccines as soon as possible." Since the FDA approved a thimerosal-free alternative of DTaP vaccine in 2001, all recommended for children (6 years of age or younger) vaccines were made available in thimerosal-free form. Trace amounts of thimerosal (<0.5 µg Hg per dose) from the manufacturing process may be found in thimerosal-free vaccines. "Given the public health goal of reducing children's exposure to mercury as much as possible, concerns have been raised about the continued presence of thimerosal in other vaccines and biological and pharmaceutical products." Further, some vaccines, which are not included in the immunization schedule for children, "still contain thimerosal as a preservative and may be given to some children" (Stratton et al., 2001). The FDA states that thimerosal (25 μg and 12.5 μg for vials appropriate for administration to children under the age 3) continues to be present in some multi-dose flu vaccines (Lillvis et al., 2014). Thimerosal also continues to be present in vaccines in a number of countries (Stratton et al., 2001).

5.2.3 Health Effects

The use of vaccines is widespread, yet "is not without risks." Generally, vaccines may cause anaphylactic shock. Polio vaccine, in particular, may, albeit rarely, cause paralytic polio while influenza vaccines are correlated with a risk of Guillain-Barre syndrome. Neurodevelopmental Disorders (NDDs) "often are recognized and diagnosed" in children after they had already received the majority of recommended vaccines (Stratton et al., 2001).

5.2.3.1 Mercury/Thimerosal

"Immune-mediated reactions to mercury-containing compounds" are "well documented in humans and in experimental animals." Exposure to mercury can have an adverse impact on the nervous system. Neurodevelopmental effects have been established for prenatal exposure to low levels of methylmercury, which is also excreted in breast milk (Stratton et al., 2001). A study conducted by the National Academy of Sciences demonstrated that chronic prenatal exposure to low doses of mercury from fish consumption is linked to "poor performance on neurobehavioral tests" and more specifically, on language, fine-motor skills, attention, visual-spatial abilities and verbal memory (Moreland, 2008). The total blood mercury levels pre-and-post vaccination with the birth dose of hepatitis B in 15 preterm and 5 control term infants were also investigated. Preterm infants "had a tenfold higher mean blood mercury level at baseline compared with term infants," yet the total blood mercury levels were elevated in both preterm and term infants (Stratton et al., 2001).

The association between autism spectrum disorder (ASD) and mercury was first established in the late 1990s and again in 2002 (Savoy, 2014). By analyzing the Vaccine Adverse Events Reporting System (VAERS) database and the 2001 U.S. Department of Education Report, a study investigated whether mercury contained in thimerosal-based vaccines contributed to neurodevelopmental disorders. "The evidence presented here shows that the occurrence of neurodevelopmental disorders following thimerosal-containing childhood vaccines does not appear to be coincidental." The study also revealed that "children received doses of mercury in their childhood vaccines that are in excess of the FDA permissible dose" (Geier & Geier, 2003). A different epidemiological study showed a 2-6 statistically significant increase in neurodevelopmental disorders after the addition of 75-100 micrograms of mercury from childhood vaccines containing thimerosal versus childhood vaccines free of thimerosal (Geier & Geier, 2003).

Last, but not least, the Immunization Safety Review Committee investigated whether the use of vaccines containing thimerosal can cause neurodevelopmental disorders (NDDs) in general and attention deficit/hyperactivity disorder (ADHD), autism and language or speech delay, in particular. The Committee confirmed the biological plausibility of the hypothesis that vaccines containing thimerosal are correlated with NDDs. Researchers have demonstrated that exposure to high doses of thimerosal is associated with neurological damage (Stratton et al., 2001).

5.2.3.2 Ethylmercury

Though "little is known about ethylmercury" and "data on the comparative toxicology of ethyl- and methylmercury are limited," a number of studies exploring the health effects of ethylmercury have led to the "thought" that many of the toxic features of ethylmercury are likely similar to the toxic effects of methylmercury (Stratton et al., 2001).

5.2.4 Legal Aspect

Children receiving standard or required immunization began experiencing adverse side effects in the 1980s. Such included, but were not limited to rash, diarrhea, colitis, hypoglycemia and shock-like state. Following injuries as well as some deaths resulting from standard vaccination and in light of the great number of lawsuits filed against vaccine manufacturers, vaccine manufacturers "pleaded with Congress to enact legislation addressing the vaccine industry's concerns about obtaining affordable liability insurance." The National Childhood Vaccine Injury Act was created by Congress in 1986 for two primary reasons: "an unstable and unpredictable vaccine market and the inadequacy of means for compensating those harmed by vaccines." The petitioners were afforded compensation (i.e., the National Vaccine Injury Compensation Program or NVICP in operation since 1989) by Congress upon successful proof of causal relationship between acquired vaccination and incurred injury within a set by Congress period of time. In 2002, the Southern District of Texas ruled that claims associating autism with vaccines must be brought under the NVICP and not against the manufacturers of vaccines.

The Vaccine Injury Compensation Trust Fund, "funded by a 75c excise tax on each dose of vaccine purchased," funds the NVICP Program. The Trust Fund balance had been estimated at $2.5 billion. 2,832 cases not related to autism were heard by NVICP since its inception. The most common cases involved injuries related to the MMR (measles-mumps-rubella), DTP (diphtheriatetanus-whole cell pertussis) and OPV (oral polio) vaccines. 1,154 cases were dismissed with attorney fees only compensated for 54 of these cases while the families who filed the remaining of the cases were compensated a total of over $819 million dollars. 5,234 autism-related cases were filed since 1999, yet none of the families who have filed such cases have been compensation as of yet. "The NVICP could be bankrupt if petitioners in autism cases are given compensation through the Program.".

In response to the large number of cases claiming autism as the resulting injury associated with vaccines and particularly the vaccines for Hepatitis B, Hemophilus Influenza Type B (HIB), Measles-Mumps-Rubella, Diphtheria-Tetanus-Pertussis, Diphtheria-Tetanus-acellar Pertussis (DTaP), The Omnibus Autism Proceedings was established as a process during which the Office of Special Masters (OSM) would hear all claims related to autism as a group. "Currently, almost 5,000 cases are being voluntarily stayed until the Omnibus Autism Proceeding concludes and determines whether a connection is established between autism and vaccines" while the number of filed cases related to autism as caused by vaccines continues to grow. 2,400 new cases associated with autism-related injuries from vaccines were filed in 2003 alone (Moreland, 2008).

Discussion

DTP is proposed to have been the only infant vaccine containing thimerosal prior to 1991. The scope of childhood vaccines containing thimerosal broadened by 1997 and by 1999, more than 30 childhood vaccines contained thimerosal. The incidence of autism in children increased from 1 in 2,500 in the mid-1980s to 1 in 300 children in 1996 and continued to rise. Such rise in the prevalence of autism is a direct reflection of the exponential growth of thimerosal-containing vaccines. Adding the facts that: a) excessive amounts of thimerosal were found in government-approved childhood vaccines; b) vaccine manufacturing corporations were not held accountable for the injury induced by their products, and c) tax money is used as a compensation for the harm caused by vaccines, confirm earlier findings that the government is (serves) the corporation while corporate profit is designed to be acquired through the dissolution of spirituality (i.e., disease).

References

Bale, J. F. (2004). Neurologic complications of immunization. *Journal of Child Neurology, 19*(6), 405-412.

Clarke, A. R., Barry, R. J., Irving, A. M., McCarthy, R. & Selikowitz, M. (2011). Children with attention-deficit/hyperactivity disorder and autistic features: EEG evidence for comorbid disorders. *Psychiatry Research, 185*, 225-231.

Geier, D. A. & Geier, M. R. (2003). An assessment of the impact of thimerosal on childhood neurodevelopmental disorders. *Pediatric Rehabilitation, 6*(2), 97-102.

Jones, W. & Klin, A. (2013). Attention to eyes is present but in decline in 2–6-month-old infants later diagnosed with autism. *Nature, 504*, 427-443.

Kalkbrenner, A. E., Schmidt, R. J., Penlesky, A. C. (2014). Environmental chemical exposures and autism spectrum disorders: A review of the epidemiological evidence. *Current Problems in Pediatric and Adolescent Health Care, 44,* 277-318.

Lillvis, D. F., Kirkland, A. & Frick, A. (2014). Power and persuasion in the vaccine debates: An analysis of political efforts and outcomes in the United States, 1998-2012. *The Milbank Quarterly, 92*(3), 475-508.

Markoulakis, R., Scharoun, S. M., Bryden, P. J. & Fletcher, P. C. (2012). An examination of handedness and footedness in children with high functioning autism and asperger syndrome. *Journal of Autism and Developmental Disorders, 42,* 2192-2201.

Meilleur, A.-A. S. & Fombonne, E. (2009). Regression of language and non-language skills in pervasive developmental disorders. *Journal of Intellectual Disability Research, 53*(2), 115-124.

Moreland, R. (2008). National Vaccine Injury Compensation Program: The potential impact of *Cedillo* for vaccine-related autism cases. *The Journal of Legal Medicine, 29,* 363-380.

O'Dwyer, L., Tanner, C., van Dongen, E. V., Greven, C. U., Bralten, J., Zwiers, M. P., Franke, B., Oosterlaan, J. Heslenfeld, D., Hoekstra, P., Hartman, C. A., Rommelse, N., & Buitelaar, J. K. (2014). Brain volumetric correlates of autism spectrum disorder symptoms in attention deficit/hyperactivity disorder. *PLOS One, 9*(6), 1-13.

Pinborough-Zimmerman, J., Bakian, A. V., Fombonne, E., Bilder, D., Taylor, J. & McMahon, W. M. (2012). Changes in the administrative prevalence of autism spectrum disorders: Contribution of special education and health from 2002-2008. *Journal of Autism and Developmental Disorders, 42,* 521-530.

Safran, S. P. (2008). Why youngsters with autistic spectrum disorders remain underrepresented in special education. *Remedial and Special Education, 29*(2), 90-95.

Savoy, M. (2014). Autism: 5 misconceptions that can complicate care. *The Journal of Family Practice, 63*(6), 310-314.

Stratton, K., Gable, A. & McCormick, M. C. (2001). Immunization safety review: Thimerosal-containing vaccines and neurodevelopmental disorders. *National Academy Press*, 1-122.

Trasande, L. (2014). Environmental contributors to autism: The pediatrician's role. *Current Problems in Pediatric and Adolescent Health Care*, 319-320.

Yassa, H. A. (2014). Autism: A form of lead and mercury toxicity. *Environmental Toxicology and Pharmacology, 38*, 1016-1024.

Chapter 6

CHILD MALTREATMENT

Based on findings generated by the World Health Organization (WHO, 2006), about 40 million children are abused worldwide every year (Connolly et al., 2010). According to U.S. estimates, more than 1 million children are "maltreated" annually (Nikulina & Widom, 2013). 2009 U.S. data reveals that 702,000 children were victims of maltreatment, 255,418 or 36% of whom "were subsequently placed in foster care" (Yampolskaya & Chuang, 2012). Emotional neglect and abuse constitute 52% and 36% of child maltreatment cases, respectively. Emotional neglect and abuse fall under the category of psychological maltreatment (PM), defined as: "a repeated pattern of caregiver behavior or a serious incident that transmits to the child that s/he is worthless, flawed, unloved, unwanted, endangered, or only of value in meeting another's needs" (Spinazzola et al., 2014).

"Consequences of child abuse and neglect have included psychiatric disorders, health risk behaviors, poor physical health, criminal behavior, and academic underachievement and lower IQ" (Nikulina & Widom, 2013). According to research findings, between 50% and 80% of children who were victims of maltreatment "experience emotional disorders and developmental delays and have other indications of behavioral problems" (Yampolskaya & Chuang, 2012). It has been further scientifically hypothesized that child neglect or abuse have a "detrimental effect on brain development leading to neurobiological alterations" (Nikulina & Widom, 2013).

6.1 Technology

138

6.1.1 Electronic Games

Electronic games may contribute to internalizing problems in children (i.e., anxiety; depression) as they take away "opportunities for growth and development, displacing face-to-face and group socializing and imaginative play." Electronic games based on violence may further result in externalizing problems in children (i.e., aggression) as they may teach them that "using virtual violence is an acceptable way to achieve goals...Previous research provides some basis for these concerns, suggesting that gaming may be linked to negative psychosocial indicators such as increased levels of hyperactivity, hostile attribution and cognition, as well as some laboratory-based measures of aggressive behavior and desensitization to risky behavior" (Przybylski, 2014). Experimental studies have lastly demonstrated that food advertisements within games have an impact on children's choice and consumption of snacks. Findings from a study reveal increases in sugar-sweetened beverages (SSBs) and decreases in fruit and vegetables (FVs) "between baseline and computers/games" (Falbe et al., 2014).

6.1.2 Television

A growing trend towards single-parent families and families in which both parents are employed "have left a void in children's lives...irresponsibly filled...by television companies and their advertisers." According to Garbarino (1995), television constitutes a part of a "socially toxic environment" within which a great number of children grow up. "He cites powerful evidence linking television to the growth of violence in children and society" (Moore, 1997). Longitudinal research has further established a "a causal link between television viewing and unhealthy weight gain in youth." The hypothesis that television viewing impacts diet (i.e., "unconscious eating;" fast-food and soda advertisements), has generated scientific support (Falbe et al., 2014).

6.2 Verbal Deception and Shaming

A study found that children who had witnessed a parent's death and who, despite efforts to convince them that what they had observed had been erroneous (i.e., a girl who had seen the body of her father hanging was told that her father had died in an auto accident) continued to trust their own senses, were ridiculed and told that the they were confusing their parent's death with a scene watched on TV. "This kind of verbal deception and shaming" contributed to "a radical mistrust of their own experience...manifesting in these cases in dissociation and severe psychiatric disturbance" (Dykstra, 2012).

6.3 Homelessness

1 to 1.3 million young people are homeless. "Homeless youth are subjected to many stressors in childhood, including lack of consistent parental care and risk for physical, sexual, and emotional abuse, that can lead to long-lasting psychological impairment...The prevalence of mental health disorders in this population is significantly higher than the national average." (Schussel & Miller, 2013).

Schussel and Miller (2013) investigated the effects of the Best Self Visualization Method (i.e., breathing; meditation; loving-kindness; sound entrainment; visualization of an idealized self) as a complement to group therapy on at-risk youth at a homeless shelter. Overall findings revealed significant effects of the Best Self Visualization Method on the well-being (i.e., positive emotional state) of homeless youth.

6.4 Paedophilia and Paedophilic Disorder

Paedophilia is commonly defined as "an adult sexual responsiveness towards immature (prepubescent) subjects" and is distinguished from paedophilic disorder, defined as "recurrent, intense sexually arousing fantasies, and sexual urges towards prepubescent children." A diagnosis of paedophilic disorder requires that such sexual urges result in significant distress, difficulties in interpersonal relationships or sexual acts involving children. Paedophilia does not require therapy as it does not result in distress, difficulties in interpersonal relationships or sexual acts involving prepubescent children. However, preventative measures could be suggested as paedophilia may serve as a risk factor for a future offense.

"Due to the lack of epidemiological studies, the exact prevalence of paedophilia is unknown." The author cites only two studies aiming to estimate the prevalence of paedophilia. Findings revealed a prevalence rate between 0.3-3.8%. The aetiology of paedophilia is not known, yet is thought to encompass biological (i.e., neurodevelopmental abnormalities), psychosocial and environmental factors. Two studies further found genetic underpinnings for the development of paedophilia. Several reports suggested that having had been sexually abused as a child increased the risk for developing paedophilia, yet the mechanism by which sexually abused children develop paedophilic interest is unknown. Imitation as well as "the facilitation of attitudes and beliefs supporting adult-child-sex" comprise two theoretical explanations (Mohnke et al., 2014).

6.5 Child Sexual Abuse (CSA)

"In Canada, children and youth account for 61% of all reported sexual assaults and 21% of all physical assaults" (Connolly et al., 2010).

***

"Child sexual abuse (CSA) has been defined as 'contacts or interactions between a child and an adult [or older child/adolescent] when the child is being used for the sexual stimulation of the perpetrator or another person'...sexual abuse involves the exploitation of children's naïveté, trust, and obedience." Findings from several studies demonstrated high frequency of CSA in the U.S. One study found that there were 78,188 confirmed incidents of child molestation in the U.S in 2003. A different study revealed that 1 in 4 girls and 1 in 6 boys are sexually abused in the U.S. prior to their 18th birthday (Wurtele, 2008). "A recent meta-analysis found that child sexual abuse (CSA) has affected as many as 25.3% of women in the United States (Lamoureux et al., 2012). About 15% of adult men report having had been sexually abused as children (Easton et al., 2013). "Although once considered a rare or nonexistent social problem, the sexual abuse of boys is gaining recognition as a public health problem...Some of that awareness has stemmed from national news coverage of sexual abuse scandals within well-established institutions (i.e., Catholic Church, the Boys Scouts of America) and universities (i.e., Penn State; Boyle, 1994; Roman Catholic Church Sexual Abuse, 2011)." A 1996 Department of Justice report showed that the sexual abuse and rape of children costs the U.S. $23 billion each year (Wurtele, 2008).

CSA has consistently been linked with poor mental and physical health outcomes for adult women, including depression, posttraumatic stress disorder (PTSD), anger, physical symptoms, and medical diagnoses." CSA survivors are also at an increased risk of contracting a sexually transmitted disease due to compromised "intimate interpersonal functioning" resulting from the trauma (Lamoureux et al., 2012).

6.6 Sexual Grooming

"The use of the Internet" (i.e., communication and collaboration between pedophile communities; exchange of child pornography; locating children for purposes of sexual abuse; desensitization; solicitation) "by individuals who seek to initiate contact with children for sexual purposes is of concern and requires attention." A "rising number of children" report "experiences of sexual solicitation and exposure to sexually explicit material" online (Kloess et al., 2014).

***

"Sexual grooming refers to the process whereby an offender prepares a child for sexual abuse… literature on this specific area is sparse considering the rapidly increasing number of incidents of adults using the Internet to befriend and exploit children in various ways (e.g., for sexual gratification, production and distribution of images of a sexually explicit nature, and contact that may facilitate or lead to sexual offenses)…Despite the significance of sexual grooming in the onset of sexual abuse, academic research has largely ignored this process."

A study conducted by Ybarra, Leaf, and Diener-West (2004) found that 97% of children and adolescents between the ages of 12 and 18 used the Internet in the U.S. 20% of these youth had "received online sexual solicitations between 1999 and 2000." 95% of 12-16 and 82% of 9-11-year-old children and adolescents used the Internet in Sweden in 2006. 32% of these youth reported having had received online sexual solicitations. "The increase in problematic or negative experiences online, and receiving of sexual solicitations, illustrates the level of prevalence of intended contact seeking and potential sexual exploitation. These figures, however, may still be a severe underrepresentation of the problem."

"A key variable in the grooming process, widely referred to across the literature, is the building, and subsequent abuse, of trust...Specific goals include gaining access to the child, gaining the child's compliance and maintaining the child's secrecy to avoid disclosure." Risk factors associated with sexual grooming of children include impaired relationships with peers and parents, school problems, bullying, immaturity, low self-esteem, behavioral and emotional difficulties. "Once an offender has identified a potential victim, they may proceed by becoming integrated in a particular community or society, adapting roles in positions of trust and in close proximity to children." Building trusting relationships with the child's support network, disguising themselves as charming to the child, giving presents to the child and desensitizing children to sexual explicit material and behavior are strategies used by child offenders to solicit a child. "Offenders may also employ coercive strategies in order to retain a child's compliance." Online solicitation may involve the offender posing as a child and initiating a conversation with the child (Kloess et al., 2014).

6.7 Trafficking

The Palemo Protocol defines child trafficking as "the act of recruitment, transportation, transfer, harboring, or receipt of a child for the purpose of exploitation, regardless of the use of illicit means, either within or outside a country. Exploitation includes prostitution and other forms of sexual exploitation, forced labor or services, slavery or practices similar to slavery, servitude, or the removal of organs." A human being who has not reached the age of 18 is referred to as a child.

Despite the passing of the Universal Declaration on Human Rights prohibiting slavery, "child trafficking, including commercial sexual exploitation (CSE), is one of the fastest growing and most lucrative criminal activities in the world." According to estimates, after the illegal trade of drugs and arms, human trafficking is the third most lucrative criminal activity in the world, estimated to generate $32 billion every year. "No region of the world" is "free of the practice." Due to factors such as varied operational definitions of child trafficking and "uncoordinated data collection and statistics riddled with methodological problems...the exact number of people who are trafficked annually worldwide is not known. Available data are elusive, confusing, and unreliable." According to 2012 International Labour Organization (ILO) estimates, 20.9 million people are forced into labor at any time, 5.5 million of whom are minors (below 18) and 22% of whom are forced into sexual exploitation. 10% are "victims of state-imposed forced labor (e.g. in prisons)," 33% of whom are minors. ILO estimates contradict sharply to 2009 United Nations Office on Drugs and Crime (UNODC) estimates, which reveal that 79% of trafficked human beings are children trafficked for CSE.

98% of those trafficked for CSE are girls and women. 12-16-year-old girls are at highest risk of being trafficked while trafficked individuals have "little or no opportunity to shake off their bondage." Internationally trafficked children are threatened with imprisonment for crimes such as illegal immigration as a preventative measure for potential escape while others who have tried to escape "have been severely beaten or killed by traffickers; many children never see their families again."

Generally, "traffickers target those who are most vulnerable, because they are easier to control." Belonging to an ethnic minority group, lack of academic credentials, compromised family support, living in rural areas or on the streets, having had run away from home due to circumstances such as family neglect or abuse and having had migrated are risk factors associated with CSE. Children living in "'out of home' placements-including youth shelters, group homes, and foster care facilities" are also at a greater risk of being trafficked.

Some children are provided with false documentation and deceived or lured "into leaving their homes with the promise of good employment opportunities. Upon arrival at their destination, they learn that they were misinformed about what awaited them; their passports are confiscated, and they are forced to work under conditions of slavery." Other children are trafficked during their course of migration, especially international migration. A third method of recruitment for CSE is called "lover boy" wherein girls are seduced and subsequently exploited. "It is the element of coercion, deception, and exploitation resulting in victims being subjected to exploitation of services or slavery that characterizes trafficking." Finally, "some families sell their children out of desperation to pay for food or health care."

"A range of individuals and groups contribute to the trafficking of children, including… corrupt officials in law enforcement, immigration, and the judicial system who have been lax in enforcing laws because of their own profiting from the illegal sex trade…Unfortunately, traffickers and their accomplices are seldom investigated, prosecuted, convicted, and punished…Facilitators of child trafficking and exploiters of children often operate with impunity because of weak or ineffective laws. One explanation often cited for the lack of enforcement of laws is the corruption among public officials and police, bribery, and public officials' active participation as brothel customers." A strong and enforced legal framework is therefore a recommended for the prevention of CSE strategy.

Reports of individuals who have assisted thousands of human trafficking victims for a number of years "suggest that the impact on children cannot be overstated." Health and safety standards have been depicted as "extremely low." Long working hours, exposure to toxins or dangerous equipment, extreme forms of violence such as physical, emotional, psychological and sexual abuse (including rape), threats to harm the victim or the victim's family and friends, communicable disease, sleep or food deprivation, social isolation, confinement, "monopolization of perception," debt bondage and confiscation of identification documentation have been identified as strategies used to "control victims." Child maltreatment has been linked to "emotional problems, aggressive behavior, substance abuse, and suicide." Physical and mental health problems have been consistently reported by trafficked for CSE girls and women (i.e., sleep disturbances; dizziness; tuberculosis; poor reproductive functioning; drug and alcohol abuse; sexually transmitted diseases; anxiety; PTSD and depression). One of the pillars around which the United Nations (UN) High Commissioner for Human Rights devised the Recommended Principles and Guidelines on Human Rights and Human Trafficking is "the prevention of trafficking by addressing root causes."

"National child protection agencies and systems designed to protect children from trafficking frequently perform ineffectively or fail to function altogether." Building strong communities (i.e., protecting and supporting children) is therefore essential in preventing CSE. International collaboration is also a vital component in the prevention of CSE. "Children who have experienced child trafficking or CSE...are a valuable resource for those who are implementing preventive interventions and should be a primary source of information on which to base programs and policies." Poverty being identified as a risk factor for CSE implies that the implementation of policies designed to reduce poverty are "vital to achieving major and sustainable progress in tackling child trafficking and CSE" (Rafferty, 2013).

Discussion

147

Substantial evidence links mainstream education to child trafficking and exploitation. First, the educational system is directly responsible for risk factors associated with child trafficking, namely vulnerability, "lack of academic credentials" and "having had run away from home due to circumstances such as family neglect or abuse." Through the removal of essential to the well-being curriculum subjects (i.e., arts; physical education), confining learning and expression to clearly delineated knowledge and skills, instilling fear (i.e., test anxiety; fear appeals) and imposing harsh consequences for failure to comply with expectations (i.e., punishment; unemployment; impaired interpersonal relationships), the educational system creates vulnerabilities, compromises academic achievement and sets the antecedents for parents to continue the trend of "neglect and abuse" via transmitting to their children that they are "worthless, flawed, unloved, unwanted, endangered, or only of value in meeting another's needs."

Second, the findings that: a) the stated goal of mainstream education is corporate profit while "child trafficking, including commercial sexual exploitation (CSE), is one of the fastest growing and most lucrative criminal activities in the world;" b) the educational system prepares youth strictly for corporate involvement while corporations "do not seem to have the ethical or spiritual sensitivity to use this power wisely, sparingly, or for the good of the whole" (*Earth, 2.31*); c) the government under which the educational system operates is directly involved in child trafficking (i.e., "corrupt officials in law enforcement, immigration, and the judicial system who have been lax in enforcing laws because of their own profiting from the illegal sex trade...one explanation often cited for the lack of enforcement of laws is the corruption among public officials and police, bribery, and public officials' active participation as brothel customers"); d) "sexual abuse scandals within...universities" (i.e., Penn State) have been recorded; e) the educational system directly leads to "risk factors associated with sexual grooming of children (i.e., "impaired relationships with peers and parents, school problems, bullying, immaturity, low self-esteem, behavioral and emotional difficulties;" f) "academic research has largely ignored" the "process" of sexual grooming leading to literature concerning sexual grooming being "sparse," provide additional robust support for the fact that mainstream education is an active participant in the grooming process of children for purposes of trafficking and exploitation.

References

Connolly, D. A., Price, H. L. & Gordon, H. M. (2010). Judicial decision making in timely and delayed prosecutions of child sexual abuse in Canada. *Psychology, Public Policy, and Law*, *16*(2), 177-199.

Dykstra, R. C. (2012) Unrepressing the kingdom: Pastoral theology as aesthetic imagination, *Pastoral Psychology*, *61*, 391-409.

Easton, S. D., Saltzman, L. Y., & Willis, D. G. (2013). "Would You Tell Under Circumstances Like That?": Barriers to disclosure of child sexual abuse for men. *Psychology of Men & Masculinity*, 1-10.

Falbe, J., Willett, W. C., Rosner, B., Gortmaker, S. L., Sonneville, K. R. & Field, A. E. (2014). Longitudinal relations of television, electronic games, and digital versatile discs with changes in diet in adolescents. *The American Journal of Clinical Nutrition*, 1173-1181.

Kloess, J. A., Beech, A. R. & Harkins, L. (2014). Online child sexual exploitation: Prevalence, process, and offender characteristics. *Trauma, Violence, & Abuse*, *15*(2), 126-139.

Lamoureux, B. E., Palmieri, P. A., Jackson, A. P. & Hobfoll, S. E. (2012). Child sexual abuse and adulthood-interpersonal outcomes: Examining pathways for intervention. *Psychological Trauma: Theory, Research, Practice, and Policy, 4*(6), 605-613.

Mohnke, S., Muller, S., Amelung, T., Kruger, T. H. C., Ponseti, J., Schiffer, B., Walter, B., Beier, K. M. & Walter, H. (2014). Brain alterations in paedophilia: A critical review. *Progress in Neurobiology, 122*, 1-23.

Moore, C. R. (1997). The need for nature: A childhood right. *Social Justice, 24*(3), 203-220.

Nikulina, V. & Widom, C. Z. (2013). Child maltreatment and executive functioning in middle adulthood: A prospective examination. *Neuropsychology, 27*(4), 417-427.

Przybylski, A. K. (2014). Electronic gaming and psychosocial adjustment. *Pediatrics, 134*(3), 716-722.

Rafferty, Y. (2013). Child trafficking and commercial sexual exploitation: A review of promising prevention policies and programs. *American Journal of Orthopsychiatry, 83*(4), 559-575.

Schussel, L. & Miller, L. (2013). Best self visualization method with high-risk youth. *Journal of Clinical Psychology, 69*(8), 836-845.

Spinazzola, J., Hodgdon, H., Liang, L.-J., Ford, J. D., Layne, C. M., Pynoos, R., Briggs, E. C., Stolbach, B. & Kisiel, C. (2014). Unseen wounds: The contribution of psychological maltreatment to child and adolescent mental health and risk outcomes. *Psychological Trauma: Theory, Research, Practice, and Policy, 6*(1), 18-28.

Wurtele, S. K. (2008). Behavioral approaches to educating young children and their parents about child sexual abuse prevention. *Journal of Behavior Analysis of Offender and Victim: Treatment and Prevention, 1*(1), 52-64.

Yampolskaya, S. & Chuang, E. (2012). Effects of mental health disorders on the risk of juvenile justice system involvement and recidivism among children placed in out-of-home care. *American Journal of Orthopsychiatry, 82*(4), 585-593.

Chapter 7

JUSTICE SYSTEM

Crimes exert a deleterious impact on victims, their families, perpetrators' families and the general public (Sawyer & Borduin, 2011). The number of incarcerated individuals is increasing in a number of countries globally. With imprisonment rate of 756 per 100,000 and 1.5 million prison population in 2009, the U.S. ranks as the country with the highest imprisonment rate and "the largest prison population" worldwide (Murray et al., 2012). "With the widening trend toward privatization of prisons, the business of corrections has stood out as a reliable growth sector in the American economy" (Barbarin, 2010). The total U.S. economic cost of "a single lifetime of crime ranges from $1.3 to $1.5 million" and includes criminal justice costs as well as the harmful outcomes associated with crime (Sawyer & Borduin, 2011). The annual U.S. economic impact of sexual assaults (including victim treatment) exceeds $1 billion (Borduin et al., 2009).

7.1 Juvenile Justice System

"There is a critical need for treatments" designed to prevent or diminish the crimes committed by serious youth offenders (Sawyer & Borduin, 2011).

***

Between 2010 and 2011, about 7.6 million people in the U.S. were "violently victimized" (Milaniak & Widom, 2014). Adolescence is the period of most heightened criminal and victimization activity (Osborne, 2004). Almost 20% of crimes are committed by individuals younger than 18 years of age

(Tackett et al., 2005). The past decade was marked by an increase in the occurrence of serious crime committed by male adolescents (Chamberlain & Reid, 1998). "Arrests for sexual offenses are relatively rare." About 20% of sexual assault arrests consist of youth under the age of 18 years old while approximately 92% of youth sexual offenders also engage in committing non-sexual crimes. Approximately 50% of all adult sexual offenders commit their initial sexual assault during adolescence (Borduin et al., 2009). Between 47% and 90% of adolescent and young adult sexual offenders have also committed nonsexual crimes. Recidivist rates for sexual crimes committed by adolescents and young adults range between 4% and 20% while the recidivist rate for nonsexual crimes committed by adolescents and young adults range between 30% and 45% at 4 to 5-year follow-up. Recidivism among adults range from 5% to 18% for sexual crimes and 36% to 68% for nonsexual crimes at 4-5-year follow-up (Ronis & Borduin, 2013). Serious youth offenders persevere to commit crime into adulthood and face a number of risks such as educational, mental, physical, financial and interpersonal difficulties (Sawyer & Borduin, 2011).

7.1.1 Correctional Boot Camps

Correctional boot camps for youth "incorporate elements of military basic training in the daily schedule" (i.e., required military-type uniforms; march; participation in "military-style drill and ceremony"). "Critics...argue" that "some aspects of the boot camps are diametrically opposed to the constructive, interpersonally supportive treatment environment necessary for positive change to occur...boot camps hold inconsistent philosophies and procedures, set the stage for abusive punishments, and perpetuate a 'we versus they' attitude suggesting newer inmates are deserving of degrading treatment" (Styve et al., 2000).

7.1.2 ODD/CD

Oppositional defiant disorder (ODD) is defined by the *Diagnostic and Statistical Manual of Mental Disorders,* 4th edition (*DSM–IV*; American Psychiatric Association, 1994) as "a recurrent pattern of negativistic, defiant, disobedient, and hostile behavior toward authority figures" (Rowe et al., 2010). Between 2% and 16% of children have been diagnosed with ODD, 52% of whom "still have the disorder" 3 years following the initial diagnosis (del Valle et al., 2001). ODD is often regarded as a "milder form of conduct disorder" (CD) "that forms an early stage in CD development" (Rowe et al., 2010). Between 81% and 91% of incarcerated youth have been diagnosed with CD (Apsche et al., 2005). "CD is marked by the child's violation of...societal norms and rules that are considered appropriate for the child's developmental age" (del Valle et al., 2001).

7.1.3 Juvenile Court

As high as 42% of "justice-involved youth...report contact with the child welfare system or child protective services" (Dierkhising et al., 2014).

***

Juvenile court systems were established as a way to both distinguish between young and adult criminal offenders and process youth offenders less punitively and with greater degree of forgiveness compared to adult offenders. Such separation in processing was based upon a common understanding that youth's developmental immaturity renders them as "less blameworthy than adults...more amendable to treatment," with "diminished decision-making skills" and "different service needs."

One of the most prominent debates in the juvenile justice system pertains as to whether youth who commit a felony should be regarded as adults due to the serious nature of the crime or as minors as per their age at the time the crime was committed (Bechtold & Cauffman, 2014). The 1980s and early 1990s were marked by concerns regarding an increase in the frequency and kind of crimes committed by youth, "portrayals of juvenile offenders as vicious 'superpredators'" and convictions that juvenile courts are not adequately capable of rehabilitating juvenile offenders. Such antecedents resulted in "a series of harsh policies." Recently, all states in the United States "have lowered the age of automatic adult prosecution below 18 for an expanded range of offenses" (Beyer, 2006). Other policies included broadening the type of crimes for which youth could be transferred to adult judicial court and allowing "prosecutors considerable discretion in adjudicating juvenile cases...Public opinion at the time generally favored these punitive measures, particularly for youths charged with serious violent or property crimes." Such policies have had a direct consequence on the way youth are sentenced. "To date, approximately 2,500 juveniles have been sentenced to life without parole, and many thousands more have received virtual life sentences (e.g., three consecutive life sentences)." According to findings from recent research, the public believes that juvenile offenders are to be held accountable for their actions. Yet, people also "favor policies that acknowledge diminished responsibility in adolescence and that provide opportunities for rehabilitation" (Greene & Evelo, 2013).

7.1.3.1 Youth Mental Health

"Knowledge of preincarceration experiences of abuse among youth in the juvenile justice system continues to grow." A large number of studies have demonstrated emotional and social problems resulting from child maltreatment. Research investigating the "cycle of violence" has revealed "consistent relation between child maltreatment and arrest as juvenile...More generally, child maltreatment is associated with delinquent behaviors...A history of child maltreatment is a robust predictor of later involvement in the juvenile justice system." On probation or detained juvenile offenders have reported "high rates of lifetime exposure to physical abuse (39.9%), neglect (30.1%), and sexual abuse (24.3%)." Up to as many of 70% of youth in juvenile facilities meet the criteria for a psychological disorder while a great number suffer from a comorbid mental condition (Dierkhising et al., 2014). A number of studies have demonstrated that juvenile offenders report high rates of traumatic experiences and posttraumatic symptoms. Research revealed that 75% or more of delinquent juvenile offenders "have experienced traumatic victimization" (Rosenberg et al., 2014).

Juvenile court youth "are disproportionally likely to have mental health issues and the stress of incarceration accentuates these problems" (Monahan et al., 2011). Researchers have demonstrated the deleterious impact of stress on mental and physical well-being (Shapiro et al.). "Experiencing stressful life events increase the risk of later developing anxiety and depressive disorders" (Chou et al., 2014). Juvenile court youth "often report mental health problems," 28-48% of which pertain to affective disorders. Stressful experiences and no social support are two critical risk factors for depressive symptoms, placing "newly incarcerated youth at an increased risk for developing internalizing problems." The beginning stage of incarceration "has been characterized as stressful and has been associated with higher levels of mental health problems (e.g., depression and anxiety) than later periods of incarceration." Depression among juvenile court youth has been associated to "substance abuse, self-harm, and in more extreme cases suicide/mortality." Concurrent stressors, including "separation from family and adjusting to a new restrictive environment" may contribute to intensified existing behavioral and emotional problems (Monahan et al., 2011).

7.1.3.2 Juvenile Court Sanctions

"Juvenile court sanctions are intended to serve the best interest of the child and to direct focus on rehabilitation." More specifically, the goal of juvenile court sanctions is to "reintegrate" youth offenders "into society" while disengaging from "delinquent behaviors." Reintegration is accomplished through "individualized case management programs" offered within the boundaries of juvenile correctional facilities (Bechtold & Cauffman, 2014). "Historically, mental health and juvenile justice services have had little success in ameliorating the serious antisocial behavior of youths." Serious youth offenders are at increased risk of substance abuse, physical and mental health problems, "interpersonal difficulties," low academic and vocational achievement (Schaeffer & Borduin, 2005). "From the early 1990s, there has been large-scale cut-backs in prison vocational and education programs in the United States, as well as reduced parole supervision, which means that inmates are left more idle in prison and have fewer prospects for employment on release" (Murray et al., 2012).

7.1.3.3 Transfer to Adult Justice System

The option of juvenile transfer to adult criminal justice system has existed "since the establishment of the juvenile court...Juveniles who commit offenses that are 'heinous or of an aggravated character, or - even though less serious - if it represents a pattern of repeated offenses which indicate that the juvenile may be beyond rehabilitation under juvenile court procedures, or if the public needs the protection afforded by such action,'" are the ones being transferred to adult criminal justice system. A number of researchers "estimate" that nearly 250,000 minors are transferred to the adult criminal justice system every year in the United States, yet "national data sets that monitor the exact number of youth transferred to adult court do not exist.".

"The decision to transfer certain juvenile offenders to adult court jurisdiction is not derived from the desire to "rehabilitate" these youths; it is a decision based primarily on the communities' and the governing bodies' desire to punish serious criminals and protect their citizens." While there are unlimited possibilities as to which adult correctional facility a youth will be housed in before or after criminal trial, "there is little empirical data to inform this decision" (Bechtold & Cauffman, 2014). During transfer hearings in the majority of states, it is the responsibility of the judge to determine whether incarceration in a juvenile correctional facility, usually until the age of 21, will protect the public. The judge must also decide on the rehabilitation of the juvenile offender. The youth's psychologist or psychiatrist may be questioned as to whether "the young person premeditated the offense, will be "cured" by age 21 with juvenile services, and will reoffend." Even when the youth is found to be "too immature to make informed choices, courts lack a competency standard relevant to juveniles...It is not uncommon for transfer hearings to lack expert testimony, and most juveniles whose cases are filed directly in adult court (without a transfer hearing) do not have expert testimony prior to or at the sentencing hearing." A great majority of such cases are filed in adult court "without a judge being involved in deciding whether the individual young person could be rehabilitated in the juvenile system." In 85% of such cases, the judge is not involved in making a decision as to whether to "prosecute a juvenile as an adult" (Beyer, 2006).

As mentioned earlier, in the 1990s, the age at which juvenile offenders could be tried in adult court was lowered on a nationwide level, "the range of young offenders subject to adult adjudication and punishment" was expanded while "the severity of penalties available to the juvenile court increased. These legal developments raise an important issue that has received surprisingly little attention: whether youths charged with crimes have the developmental capacities needed to participate effectively in their trials." A criminal proceeding is in accordance with constitutional requirements solely in instances when the defendant is "competent to stand trial" (i.e., comprehend the criminal proceeding to an extent that allows participation). "The conventional standard that has been applied focuses on mental illness and disability...there has been little recognition that youths in criminal court may be incompetent because of developmental immaturity." Research has revealed that some youth will exhibit deficiencies in ability pertaining to legal matters as a result of developmental immaturity (Grisso et al., 2003). Study findings revealed that 50 delinquent youth in either adult or juvenile correctional facilities exhibited "the same disabilities, past trauma, and immaturity...A majority of the 50 youth had characteristics of teenagers likely to outgrow delinquency, yet more than half of them were sentenced to adult prison...Children as young as 12 are being sentenced to 20 years to life in adult prison" (Beyer, 2006).

"Housing minors in adult facilities has a history of research that has documented many harmful effects." According to researchers, juvenile offenders' exposure to adult inmates "might provide a platform from which youthful offenders develop more sophisticated criminal skills, become entrenched in the criminal culture, and become persistent offenders. Indeed, a number of researchers have demonstrated that delinquent adolescent offenders who socialize regularly "teach and reinforce one another to be more delinquent." The U.S. Department of Justice Special Report investigating the rates of recidivism amongst inmates released from adult state prison found that "the highest rates of rearrests, reconviction, and being returned to prison with a new sentence were found among 14- to 17-year-olds." 82.1% of youth inmates 14-17 years of age, 75% of offenders 18-24 years of age, 70.5% - 25-29 years of age and 66.2% of 35-39 years of age inmates were re-arrested within a period of 3 years following release from adult prison. A meta-analysis further demonstrated that the transfer of youth offenders from juvenile to adult court jurisdiction "has no deterrent value, and in fact, may actually increase subsequent antisocial behavior."

Lastly, "many youth in adult facilities experience a significant degree of physical and sexual abuse - which may account for the higher rates of suicide among youth in adult facilities compared with youth in juvenile facilities." 59 youth in juvenile and 81 – in adult correctional facilities in Boston, Memphis, Detroit and Newark were interviewed by researchers. Results revealed that 9.9% of youth in adult correctional facilities "reported being beaten up by staff (compared to 5.1% in juvenile facilities), 32.1% reported being attacked with a weapon (compared to 23.7% in juvenile facilities), 8.6 reported being sexually attacked or raped (compared to 1.7% in juvenile facilities), and 45.7% reported being violently victimized (compared to 36.7% in juvenile facilities)" (Bechtold & Cauffman, 2014).

7.1.3.4 Violations of the Eight Amendment

The Eight Amendment of the United States Constitution prohibits "punishments that are cruel and unusual." Cruel and unusual punishments are such that are not proportioned to the crime (Greene & Evelo, 2013). "Abuse during incarceration violates the civil and constitutional rights of youth" (Dierkhising et al., 2014).

***

"Our knowledge is still limited regarding what is actually happening in the facilities youth are incarcerated...Accurate data" regarding physical abuse at the time of incarceration "have been scarce given the difficulties in documenting physical abuse perpetrated by staff...Importantly, the experience of physical abuse by staff is obscured by practices that are routine and legal in juvenile facilities (e.g., handcuffing, use of force, and restraint)...Because detention staff work in a potentially unsafe environment, they are given the legal authority to use force. It is only when these practices are overused or misused that they are then classified as 'excessive use of force'...Use of force includes use of restraints, chemical agents, electronic devices and weapons...For the past 40 years, systemic violence in juvenile justice facilities has been legally documented by court records from lawsuits in the majority of states across the country. This documentation reveals, 'states have been identified not for one or a handful of isolated events, but for sustained patterns of maltreatment'...13,000 claims of physical abuse by staff were reported by youth between 2004 and 2007 across the country." Such rates were classified as "alarming." The Bureau of Justice Statistics found that formal allegations of sexual misconduct in juvenile correctional facilities "averaged around 2,000 cases a year in 2005 and 2006, with 32% classified as staff sexual misconduct, 11% as staff sexual harassment, and 57% youth-on-youth sexual violence." Between 2004 and 2007, "10.3% of youth" reported "sexual abuse by staff while incarcerated...across the country."

A recent study investigated the prevalence of abuse at the time of incarceration and evaluated the criminal behavior and mental health of "formerly incarcerated young adults." The study sample was comprised of 62 males who were first arrested between 9 and 17 years of age. The average first arrest age was estimated at 13.78 years of age. Results revealed that 96.8% of young adults experienced at least one type of abuse (i.e., vicarious; witnessed; direct), 95.2% witnessed abuse, 93.5% experienced vicarious abuse while 77.4% of formerly incarcerated young adults experienced direct abuse. One young adult recounted: "a staff picked up a kid and slammed him to the ground" while another reported: "I got my collar bone broken by staff at camp." 54.8% of young adults were subjected to solitary confinement while 54.8% - to peer physical abuse. One young adult reported: "Staff allowing fights or turning their heads" and another stated: "Lots of fights that could have been controlled…Excessive" room confinement and peer physical abuse were the two most prevalent forms of direct abuse. Psychological abuse by staff members (45.2%) was found to be the third most prevalent type of abuse during incarceration. One young adult recounted: "Some staff are unfair and use the power of the pen to verbally challenge us. In other words, power tripping." 82.3% of participants reported exposure to peer physical abuse, 70.5% - exposure to assault by staff and 66.1% - exposure to unwarranted use of room confinement. Exposure to peer and staff abuse alongside excessive use of solitary confinement were the most frequently cited types of witnessed abuse. Peer physical abuse (87.1%), physical assault by a staff member (77.4%) and unwarranted use of room confinement (71%) were the most commonly cited types of vicarious exposure. Additional responses indicative of other types of abuse included: "Many staff members were involved in gangs themselves. Some staff members would have verbal sexual harassment toward minors…Some of the staff…made us do unnecessary things." The average frequency of abuse experienced by formerly incarcerated youth was 4.73 for direct abuse, 10.07 for vicarious abuse and 7.39 for witnessed abuse. The average frequency of all types of abuse equaled 22.18. Abuse during incarceration was associated with "poor postrelease social and emotional functioning," and more specifically to posttraumatic stress, depression and criminal involvement following release. Child maltreatment was positively correlated with abuse during incarceration and adjustment problems (i.e., involvement in criminal activity; depression; posttraumatic stress) following release. 38.7% of participants experienced at least one type of child maltreatment (i.e., neglect; physical abuse; sexual abuse). 33.9% experienced mild to robust depressive symptoms while 14.5% - clinical posttraumatic stress. Direct evidence concerning emotional and social functioning following incarceration-related abuse is "scarce" (Dierkhising et al., 2014).

"Youth suicide in the community has been identified as a major public health problem in the United States... juvenile suicide in confinement has received little attention" (Hayes, 2005). The Survey of Youth in Residential Placement and the Bureau of Justice Statistics' National Survey of Youth in Custody reports were released in 2010. According to findings based on a national sample of 7.073 youth in juvenile facilities, "more than one third of youth in custody reported spending time in solitary confinement, and more than half (55%) of those youth reported solitary confinement exceeding 24 hours, which is against best practice guidelines...Prolonged stay in solitary confinement...has been linked to suicide during confinement." Based on findings from a national survey, approximately half of suicide cases among incarcerated youth had taken place during solitary confinement. A Human Rights Watch investigation revealed that "solitary confinement often triggered traumatic reminders of prior trauma." One youth participant in the investigation stated: "Once you are confined the way I was, then any other confinement just triggers that experience - loss of sleep, all these different flashbacks of different bad events. You try to harness it, but you don't know how or what's going on or what's happening."

Empirical evidence concerning abuse in juvenile correctional facilities is necessary for "policymakers to advocate on behalf of the safety of incarcerated youth." Yet, "reporting procedures (e.g., grievance policies) for youth regarding staff misconduct are often problematic, resulting in underestimation of the prevalence rates. Staff may discourage youth from submitting grievances, grievances may be destroyed or ignored, and even when submitted no formal response or consequence may be offered...A 2003 Court ruling...limited attorney compensation" which has partially resulted in "fewer lawsuits...brought against facilities" (Dierkhising et al., 2014).

7.2 Adult Justice System

The main concerns of adult court systems are "retribution and public safety" (Bechtold & Cauffman, 2014).

7.2.1 Violations of the Eight Amendment

"The existence of prison rape in male prisons in the United States is a serious problem with pervasive and devastating consequences...Such assaults are not only criminal in nature but also are crimes that take place in a facility created, funded, and operated by the state, which bears the responsibility of keeping its wards from predictable and preventable harm...Some prison staff may use the fear of sexual exploitation or may actually facilitate sexual exploitation as a method for controlling prisoners."

Sexual victimization in prison may carry serious and long-lasting implications, with potentially devastating physiological, social, and psychological components." Davis (1968) was one of the first researchers to document a 5% prevalence of sexual violence in prisons. Findings published in 1996 revealed a 1 in 10 victimization rate. The high prevalence and alarming nature of prison rape led to the 2003 passage of the Prison Rape Elimination Act (PREA), designed to prevent, identify and respond to sexual coercion in prison settings.

Risk factors associated with sexual victimization of men in prison include feminine traits, young age, small physique, bisexual or homosexual orientation, middle to upper social class, higher educational achievement, having committed a non-violent or sexual offense, history of sexual victimization, being an immigrant, being in prison for the first time, being perceived as fearful or weak, having a mental illness and being White (Neal & Clements, 2010).

7.2.2 Incarcerated Parents

"More parents than ever are behind bars." Approximately half of the U.S. prison population are parents of children younger than 18 years of age. In 2004, 67% of incarcerated parents had a substance use problem while 57% experienced a mental health problem. While "the most common current offense for inmate mothers was a drug offense (35%)...the most common offense for inmate fathers was a violent offense (45%)."

22% of children with an imprisoned parent in 2004 were 4 years of age or younger, 30% - 5-9 years of age, 32% - 10-14 and 16% - 15-17 years. The parent of more than 33.3% of these children was expected to remain imprisoned until his or her child reached 18 years of age. The parents of 950,000 U.S. children were imprisoned in 1991. This number increased to 1.7 million in 2007 or 2.3% of the country's children. According to statistics, 1 in every 25 Caucasian children and 1 in every 4 African American children born in 1990 had been subjected to parental imprisonment before they turned 14. Fathers represent 91% of incarcerated parents. The number of children with an imprisoned mother "more than doubled" between 1991 and 2007 while the number of children with an imprisoned father increased by 77% during the same period.

"The arrest of a parent can cause children to feel shocked, bewildered, and scared. Arrest often occurs at night or in the early morning, when people are likely to be at home with their families. The experience can be unexpected and sometimes involve witnessing violence." An imprisoned mother as part of an English study recalls her arrest: "the front and back door were crashed in simultaneously. The house was full of policemen with hammers looking for drugs. It was very frightening, my son was hysterical." The results of a different study involving 192 imprisoned parents in Arkansas revealed that 40% of children witnessed their arrest. Weapons were drawn in 27% of these arrest cases while law enforcement officers informed children as to the reason for the arrest of their parents in only 20% of the sample. In 97% of fathers' arrests and 70% of mothers' arrests, parents were handcuffed with the child being present at the scene. In yet another study of 36 children with imprisoned mothers, "many children had symptoms of posttraumatic stress disorder, including flashbacks of their mother's arrest." Trial in court upon parental arrest "can be highly anxiety provoking for families and children" as it compromises their ability to make future plans until a court order is reached (Murray et al., 2012).

"The forced separation imposed by imprisonment creates a unique cluster of...stresses" (i.e., matters of custody; restricted contact with their children; worry regarding the care provided to their children; lack of control and loss of identity as a mother). Approximately one half of incarcerated parents "provided the primary financial support for their children before incarceration." More than 50% of all female prisoners "are mothers of at least one child under age 18 for whom they were responsible before incarceration" (Clements, 1979). Less than half of imprisoned mothers and fathers report that their children are being cared for by someone else (i.e., foster homes; agencies; grandparents; relatives; friends) during the course of their imprisonment.

Children with detained parents can experience a number of social and emotional challenges associated with their parent's detainment, "which may develop into a range of adjustment problems in the long term" (Murray et al., 2012). "Childhood and adolescent antisocial behavior (ASB) represent a serious societal problem" (Tackett et al., 2005). According to results from a meta-analysis, "parental incarceration predicts increased risk for children's antisocial behavior." Antisocial behavior is defined as an array of behaviors violating "social norms or laws." According to findings from a study, boys who experienced parental incarceration before their 10th birthday "had about double the risk of antisocial behavior, internalizing problems, and other adverse outcomes up to age 48" (Murray et al., 2012). "Children of incarcerated parents frequently experience difficulties at school...and emotional disregulation. They are also more likely to have experienced maltreatment or abuse than children of nonincarcerated parents" (Clements, 1979). Change of caregiving circumstances which may result in "reduced quality of care" is an additional difficulty that children of incarcerated parents may experience.

Aside from a "lack of dependable and intimate contact with their incarcerated parents," inability to visit their incarcerated parent without an accompanying adult and intimidating procedures (i.e., sniffed by dogs; passing through a metal detector; being searched) associated with a visit, social stigma attached to parental incarceration may cause children to become isolated, rejected by their peers and subjected to peer hostility. Lastly, parental release may lead to "significant barriers to successful reintegration" (i.e., housing; employment) "which may impose further burdens on the family" (Murray et al., 2012).

Discussion

The findings that: a) vaccine manufacturers are not held liable for producing harmful products; b) governmental officials are actively involved in facilitating and participating in child trafficking and exploitation; c) the goal of public education is corporate profit; d) mainstream education nurtures at an ever increasing rate delinquency, aggression and psychological impairments in youth, leading to imprisonment; e) prisons are increasingly being privatized; f) in 85% of transfer hearings, the judge is not involved in making a decision as to whether to "prosecute a juvenile as an adult;" g) "the decision to transfer certain juvenile offenders to adult court jurisdiction is not derived from the desire to "rehabilitate" these youths; it is a decision based primarily on the communities' and the governing bodies' desire to punish serious criminals and protect their citizens;" h) "reporting procedures (e.g., grievance policies) for youth regarding staff misconduct are often problematic...Staff may discourage youth from submitting grievances, grievances may be destroyed or ignored, and even when submitted no formal response or consequence may be offered...A 2003 Court ruling...limited attorney compensation," partially resulting in "fewer lawsuits...brought against facilities;" i) contrary to research, punishment-based prison interventions are implemented; j) "many staff members" are "involved in gangs themselves;" k) while youth and adults are intimidated, held accountable and severely punished for their actions, manufactured by mainstream education, in particular, and the system at large, there is no accountability and consequences for prison staff rape, facilitation of sexual exploitation and excessive prison confinement – all suggest that the role of governments is to merge with corporations or facilitate the shift towards corporations taking the role of the new government.

References

Apsche, J. A., Bass, C. K., Jennings, J. L. & Siv, A. M. (2005). A review and empirical comparison of two treatments for adolescent males with conduct and personality disorder: Mode deactivation therapy and cognitive behavior therapy. *International Journal of Behavioral Consultative Therapy*, *1*(1), 27-45.

Barbarin, O. A. (2010). Halting African American boys' progression from Pre-K to prison: What families, schools, and communities can do! *American Journal of Orthopsychiatry*, *80*(1), 81-88.

Bechtold, J. & Cauffman, E. (2014). Tried as an adult, housed as a juvenile: A tale of youth from two courts incarcerated together. *Law and Human Behavior*, *38*(2), 126-138.

Beyer, M. (2006). Fifty delinquents in juvenile and adult court. *American Journal of Orthopsychiatry*, *76*(2), 206-214.

Borduin, C. M., Schaeffer, C. M. & Heiblum, N. (2009). A randomized clinical trial of multisystemic therapy with juvenile sexual offenders: Effects on youth social ecology and criminal activity. *Journal of Consulting and Clinical Psychology*, *77*(1), 26-37.

Chamberlain, P. & Reid, J. B. (1998). Comparison of two community alternatives to incarceration for chronic juvenile offenders. *Journal of Consulting and Clinical Psychology*, *66*(4), 624-633.

Chou, D., Huang, C.-C. & Hsu, K.-S. (2014). Brain-derived neurotrophic factor in the amygdala mediates susceptibility to fear conditioning. *Experimental Neurology*, *255*, 19-29.

Clements, C. B. (1979). Crowded prisons: A review of psychological and environmental effects. *Law and Human Behavior*, *3*(3), 217-225.

del Valle, P., Kelley, S. L. & Seoanes, J. E. (2001). The "Oppositional Defiant" and "Conduct Disorder" child: A brief review of etiology, assessment, and treatment. *Behavioral Development Bulletin, 1*, 36-41.

Dierkhising, C. B., Lane, A. & Natsuaki, M. N. (2014). Victims behind bars: A preliminary study of abuse during juvenile incarceration and post-release social and emotional functioning. *Psychology, Public Policy, and Law, 20*(2), 181-190.

Greene, E. & Evelo, A. J. (2013). Attitudes regarding life sentences for juvenile offenders. *Law and Human Behavior, 37*(4), 276-289.

Grisso, T., Steinberg, L., Woolard, J., Cauffman, E., Scott, E., Graham, S., Lexcen, F., Reppucci, N. D. & Schwartz, R. (2003). Juveniles' competence to stand trial: A comparison of adolescents' and adults' capacities as trial defendants. *Law and Human Behavior, 27*(4), 333-363.

Hayes, L. M. (2005). Juvenile suicide in confinement in the United States: Results from a national survey. *Crisis, 26*(3),146-148.

Milaniak, I. & Widom, C. Z. (2014). Does child abuse and neglect increase risk for perpetration of violence inside and outside the home? *Psychology of Violence*, 1-10.

Monahan, K. C., Goldweber, A. & Cauffman, E. (2011). The effects of visitation on incarcerated juvenile offenders: How contact with the outside impacts adjustment on the inside. *Law and Human Behavior, 35*, 143-151.

Murray, J., Farrington, D. P. & Sekol, I. (2012). Children's antisocial behavior, mental health, drug use, and educational performance after parental incarceration: A systematic review and meta-analysis. *Psychological Bulletin, 138*(2), 175-210.

Neal, T. M. S. & Clements, C. B. (2010). Prison rape and psychological sequelae: A call for research. *Psychology, Public Policy, and Law, 16*(3), 284-299.

Osborne, J. W. (2004). Identification with academics and violence in schools. *Review of General Psychology, 8*(3), 147-162.

Ronis, S. T. & Borduin, C. M. (2013). Antisocial behavior trajectories of adolescents and emerging adults with histories of sexual aggression. *Psychology of Violence, 3*(4), 367-380.

Rosenberg, H. J., Vance, J. E., Rosenberg, S. D., Wolford, G. L., Ashley, S. W. & Howard, M. L. (2014). Trauma exposure, psychiatric disorders, and resiliency in juvenile-justice-involved youth. *Psychological Trauma: Theory, Research, Practice, and Policy, 6*(4), 430-437.

Rowe, R., Costello, E. J., Angold, A., Copeland, W. E. & Maughan, B. (2010). Developmental pathways in oppositional defiant disorder and conduct disorder. *Journal of Abnormal Psychology, 119*(4), 726-738.

Sawyer, A. M. & Borduin, C. M. (2011). Effects of multisystemic therapy through midlife: A 21.9-year follow-up to a randomized clinical trial with serious and violent juvenile offenders. *Journal of Consulting and Clinical Psychology, 79*(5), 643-652.

Schaeffer, C. M. & Borduin, C. M. (2005). Long-term follow-up to a randomized clinical trial of multisystemic therapy with serious and violent juvenile offenders. *Journal of Consulting and Clinical Psychology, 73*(3), 445-453.

Shapiro, S. L., Schwartz, G. E. & Bonner, G. (1998). Effects of mindfulness-based stress reduction on medical and premedical students. *Journal of Behavioral Medicine, 21*(6), 581-599.

Styve, G. J., MacKenzie, D. L., Gover, A. R. & Mitchell, O. (2000). Perceived conditions of confinement: A national evaluation of juvenile boot camps and traditional facilities. *Law and Human Behavior, 24*(3), 297-308.

Tackett, J. L., Krueger, R. F., Iacono, W. G. & McGue, M. (2005). Symptom-based subfactors of *DSM*-defined conduct disorder: Evidence for etiologic distinctions. *Journal of Abnormal Psychology, 114*(3), 483-487.

Chapter 8

WAR

"Civil strife and war have become the norm in many regions of the world" (Zahr, 1996). "Social conflict is a rising problem that threatens the security and well-being of societies globally. There are over 30 wars and violent conflicts being waged around the world; approximately 40% of intrastate armed conflicts have lasted for 10 years or more, and 25% of wars have lasted for more than 25 years." Social conflict often results in division among families and communities, extreme forms of violence and mental health problems (Ho & Fung, 2011).

8.1 Psychological Impairments

"The nature, severity, and cumulative effects of direct exposure to violent events are key risk factors for developing posttraumatic stress disorder (PTSD) and other behavioral problems, including sleep disturbances, anger, aggression, depression, and anxiety. Similar findings have been documented for indirect exposure to violent events as well" (Rojas-Flores et al., 2013). 10% of people who have undergone trauma will experience significant emotional challenges and 10% "will develop problems that will interfere with their ability to function effectively." Depression and anxiety are most common following exposure to a traumatic experience (Ron, 2014).

Children become directly exposed to war-induced violent events as armed conflicts often take place in "populated civilian areas" where children comprise a large percentage of the population (Zahr, 1996). According to research findings, destruction, loss of human life and being a witness to murders have a negative impact on "children's social, cognitive, and emotional development and predict PTSD and other anxiety and mood disorders." A meta-analysis of the risk factors associated with childhood and adolescent PTSD further revealed that impaired cognitive processes were most prevalent. "Thought suppression and involuntary attention to life threats were the most dysfunctional" (Punamäki et al., 2014). Affected by war children have also been found to exhibit behavioral problems (i.e., fear of separation), sleep impairments, shift in moral values and enhanced dependence (Zahr, 1996). Youth delinquency has increased in the North American and European parts of the world following World War II (Liau et al., 2003). Lastly, war may interfere with children's normal activities such as spending time with family, attending school, engaging in play outdoors or sleeping in their personal beds (Zahr, 1996).

8.2 Childhood Emotions

Extrinsic emotion regulation implies that children learn to regulate their emotions through "affecting" the emotions and behavior of other people. Intrinsic emotion regulation, on the other hand, encompasses the manipulation of emotions such as when frightened or embarrassed. Children who have been affected by war use emotional regulation strategies such as soothing, consoling and manipulating their emotions in order to "maintain balance and adjust to overwhelmingly frightened and traumatic conditions."

"Emotions are either strangely absent or overwhelmingly present among trauma victims." Palestine's military occupation and the Gaza war exposed children to 31 events classified under 4 categories: 1) "being personally targeted by the enemy army" (i.e., being physically abused; being wounded; being burned by phosphorous bombs); 2) loss of family and friends; 3) destruction (i.e., home and home land demolition); 4) witnessing violence (i.e., seeing the death and injury of people, body parts). A study investigated whether children had experienced any such events during the war in Gaza. Results revealed that "traumatic memories of destruction, human loss, and violent scenes were still vividly present in children's minds." During the first session of a psychosocial treatment intervention, "many participants were so afraid that they could not stay alone in the room, and many continued to talk and dream about painful war experiences." Children who exhibited high emotional control limited their emotional expression, "perhaps even to the extent of suppressing them." Despite the fact that the "cessation of acute life threats provided some relief and safety, these highly controlled children could not afford to release the pressure." The authors of the research concerning children exposed to the war in Gaza proposed that less intensified emotion regulation has beneficial effects on children's mental health as it promotes their steady ability to "ease their highly taxing survival efforts" after the cessation of "acute life threats and war violence" (Punamäki et al., 2014).

8.3 Parenting

Twenty to forty thousand children have died as a direct result of armed conflicts in Lebanon while forty to eighty thousand "have been disabled or handicap." Study findings demonstrated that a number of handicapped in Lebanon do not receive necessary services due to lack of adequate resources and "medical facilities." Lebanese children exposed to armed conflicts further experienced "high levels of aggressiveness, anxiety, bed-wetting, depression, fear, grief, overactivity, overdependence, poor school performance and sleep disturbances among other symptoms." Children exposed to heavy shelling two years prior to the study experienced greater behavior problems compared to children not exposed to such conditions. A number of Lebanese mothers "felt that the demands of war make them unable to meet their children's needs and some have admitted that at times they were violent with their children" (Zahr, 1996). "In general, depression, anxiety, and PTSD stemming from exposure to violence seem to negatively affect parenting by contributing to maladaptive parent-child interactions, ineffective listening and attunement to children's distress, withdrawal, and difficulty in tolerating children's subsequent anxiety and aggression.

In aversive environments where families are exposed to high levels of CV, parents can play a crucial role in protecting or placing their children at risk for further psychological distress." Developing resilience rather psychological disorders is also a feasible outcome of a traumatic event. Evidence demonstrated that effective resolution of a traumatic experience could contribute to personal growth (Rojas-Flores et al., 2013).

8.4 Childhood Resiliency

"A number of researchers have criticized the research on "children and war" for medicalizing and psychologizing the national struggle and for ignoring the potential resources and strengths" (Peltonen et al., 2014).

***

Children and adolescents affected by war are either depicted as "highly traumatized" or as resilient, enduring and invincible. According to researchers, resilience can only emerge under adverse circumstances. Resilient youth are capable of maintaining mental balance and normal functioning level despite war-related traumatic experiences. They are even able to "blossom" or to experience "exceptionally positive outcomes despite adversity."

176

Posttraumatic growth or "positively experienced psychological change," ability to thrive and to re-adjust, are examples of "exceptionally positive outcomes." Empirical reviews demonstrated that children's optimal emotional and cognitive processes, societal and school resources, supporting and loving family environment, serve as resilience-building and mental-health protective factors among children who have been affected by war. A study found that optimism was correlated with low levels of PTSD and depressive symptoms while "perceived competence" was associated with lower levels of depression. Evidence further revealed that adequate parental support is beneficial for children's creativity, mental and developmental functioning and health.

A different study investigated the percentage of resilient children among a sample of 483 Palestinian children between the ages of 10 and 13 who were exposed to Gaza war-related atrocities such as experiencing and witnessing war violence and losing a family member or a friend. Resilient children were operationalized as having been exposed to severe war traumas, yet not exhibiting signs of PTSD. 33% of participating children were classified as resilient (i.e., high degree of war-related trauma; no PTSD), 27% were identified as traumatized (i.e., high degree of war-related trauma; evidence of PTSD), 20% - as low degree of war-related trauma and presence of PTSD and finally 20% - as low exposure to war-related trauma and no PTSD. A review of studies further demonstrated that middle-class children of favorable ethnic background who were exposed to a sole traumatic event experienced higher resiliency compared to children of ethnic minorities and low socioeconomic status who had endured a number of traumatic events. It was concluded that overall resilience among children who had experienced "severe adversity" is rarely evident (Peltonen et al., 2014).

According to Neff (2003a, 2003b), "self-compassion involves treating yourself with care and concern when considering personal inadequacies, mistakes, failures, and painful life situations." A growing body of research demonstrates that "self-compassion is an important predictor of well-being and resilience" (Smeets et al., 2014).

8.5 Military Personnel: Psychological Impairments

Soldiers experience a number of stressors at war (i.e., threat; severe living conditions; no privacy), many of which lead to mental health problems (Wood et al., 2011). "During the past decade, risk for suicide and suicide ideation among military personnel and veterans has increased. Among military personnel, suicide is now the second leading cause of death." Moral injury (i.e., causing harm to others; inability to prevent adverse outcomes) is a unique suicide risk factor among military personnel. Moral injury is associated with experiences of shame, guilt, self-deprecation and difficulties related to forgiveness. Researchers have demonstrated a link between such experiences, suicide ideation and attempt among military personnel (Bryan et al., 2014).

Discussion

The steady introduction of NCLB prior to its enactment exemplified desensitization. *Sexual Grooming* (*6.6*) further demonstrated that "desensitizing children to sexual explicit material and behavior" is a strategy "used by child offenders to solicit a child." Lastly, *Youth Mental Health* (*7.1.3.1*) revealed that the initial stages of incarceration are "associated with higher levels of mental health problems" compared to "later periods of incarceration." In line with the trend of desensitization, with more than 30 "wars and violent conflicts" worldwide, "civil strife and war have become the norm in many regions of the world" while "social conflict" is a "rising problem." War leads to severe internalizing and externalizing psychological maladjustments (i.e., anger; aggression), which subsequently serve as the antecedents to greater conflict. Greater conflict equates to dissolution of spirituality or life at an ever increasing rate.

It could be concluded that war begins with the educational system desensitizing youth to a value system of standardization, competition, division, adverse consequences associated with noncompliance, and culminates with the extinguishment of life and the acquisition of absolute corporate profit.

References

Bryan, A. O., Theriault, J. L. & Bryan, C. J. (2014). Self-forgiveness, posttraumatic stress, and suicide attempts among military personnel and veterans. *Traumatology*, 1-7.

Ho, M. Y. & Fung, H. H. (2011). A dynamic process model of forgiveness: A cross-cultural perspective. *Review of General Psychology*, *15*(1), 77-84.

Liau, A. K., Liau, A. W., Teoh, G. B. S. & Liai, M. T. L. (2003). The case for emotional literacy: The influence of emotional intelligence on problem behaviours in Malaysian secondary school students. *Journal of Moral Education, 32*(1), 51-66.

Peltonen, K., Qouta, S., Diab, M. & Punamäki, R. L. (2014). Resilience among children in war: The role of multilevel social factors. *Traumatology*, *20*(4), 232-240.

Punamäki, R.-L., Peltonen, K., Diab, M. & Qouta, S. R. (2014). Psychosocial interventions and emotion regulation among war-affected children: Randomized control trial effects. *Traumatology*, *20*(4), 241-252.

Rojas-Flores, L., Herrera, S., Currier, J. M., Lin, E. Y., Kulzer, R. & Foy, D. W. (2013). "We Are Raising Our Children in Fear": War, community violence, and parenting practices in El Salvador. *International Perspectives in Psychology: Research, Practice, Consultation, 2*(4), 269-285.

Ron, P. (2014). Posttraumatic stress disorder among three-generation families in times of war: A comparison between Israeli Jewish and Arabs after the second Lebanon War (2006) and Cast Lead Operation (2009). *Traumatology, 20*(4), 269-276.

Smeets, E., Neff, K., Alberts, H. & Peters, M. (2014). Meeting suffering with kindness: Effects of a brief self-compassion intervention for female college students. *Journal of Clinical Psychology, 70*(9), 794-807.

Wood, M. D., Britt, T. W., Thomas, J. L., Klocko, R. P. & Bliese, P. D. (2011). Buffering effects of benefit finding in a war environment. *Military Psychology, 23*, 202-219.

Zahr, L. K. (1996). Effects of war on the behavior of Lebanese preschool children: Influence of home environment and family functioning. *American Journal of Orthopsychiatry, 66*(3), 401-408.

Chapter 9

FEAR

"Fear is the most extensively studied emotion (LeDoux, 2014). Fear has been defined as "an emotional response activated in the presence of stimuli signaling upcoming danger" (Gartstein et al., 2010). According to Edward Tolman, "fear...was an intervening variable that accounted for the expression of defensive behaviors in the presence of a threat" (LeDoux, 2014). According to Rachman, verbal communication regarding a potential threat associated with a stimulus, traumatic event or an association with a traumatic event and vicarious learning (i.e., the observation of another's fear resulting from a stimulus) are three possible means by which environmental factors may lead to the experience of fear (Field & Schorah, 2007).

    "In humans, pathological forms of learned fear are hallmarks of severe psychopathologies, such as anxiety disorders, post-traumatic stress disorders (PTSD), and depression" (Kong et al., 2014). "In the case of psychiatric disorders, fear responses may persist long after the danger has passed. This persistent form of fear is a core component of many anxiety disorders, including posttraumatic stress disorder (PTSD)" (King et al., 2013). There is a strong association between fear of positive and negative evaluation, social anxiety and social anxiety disorder. According to Gilbert and colleagues (Gilbert, 2001), social anxiety serves the function of balancing the risks associated with "trying to move up a dominance hierarchy too quickly versus falling out of the hierarchy completely (i.e., being ostracized)." Negative evaluation within such context would signify a downward hierarchical slope while positive evaluation would "serve as a warning signal that the person may offend important others or be put in a position of having to defend newly-acquired status" (Rodebaugha et al., 2012).

9.1 Fear Conditioning

"Fear learning mechanisms" are "one of the most intensely studied questions in neuroscience...during the last decade, 400 papers/year have been published on this question" (Duvarci & Pare, 2014).

The way fear has most often been investigated is through Pavlovian fear conditioning" (LeDoux, 2014). "In differential Pavlovian fear conditioning, one previously neutral conditional stimulus (CS) can come to elicit a conditional response (CR) through repeated pairing with an aversive unconditional stimulus (UCS)" (Schultz & Helmstetter, 2010). Pavlovian associative learning theory has (Kong et al., 2014) "shown that an initially emotionally neutral conditioned stimulus (CS) can acquire negative affective properties on repeated pairings with an adverse unconditioned stimulus" (King et al., 2013). "In the classical paradigm...after repeated CS–US pairings, an association is formed such that presentation of the CS alone elicits the same set of behavioral and autonomic responses (conditioned responses; CR) formerly produced by the US" (Chou et al., 2014). "Fear conditioning occurs rapidly, often after few pairings of a CS with a shock US" (Abraham et al., 2014). Fear conditioning is used to explain why some individuals develop psychopathology while others are able to cope with the trauma (Chou et al., 2014).

Fear conditioning allows researchers to control the independent variables or antecedents and measure the dependent variables or the outcomes. Fear conditioning is effective as it "taps into a process called associative learning that is a feature of circuits in the nervous systems of many if not all animals and may also exist in single-cell organisms...The fear-conditioning process allows the US to alter the effectiveness of the CS in activating circuits that control defense responses in anticipation of harm…It is rapidly acquired, and is long-lasting, often persisting throughout life." Researchers have established that "conditioned or unconditioned threats presented subliminally elicit physiological responses without the person being aware of the stimulus and without reporting any particular feeling, even when instructed to try to introspect about feelings. The conditioning process can also be carried out nonconsciously and without awareness of the CS–US contingency… The function of the neural circuit that underlies fear conditioning is to coordinate brain and body resources to increase the chance of surviving the encounter predicted by the CS with minimal adverse consequences, not to make conscious fear…Conscious fear can cause us to act in certain ways, but it is not the cause of the expression of defensive behaviors and physiological responses elicited by conditioned or unconditioned threats" (LeDoux, 2014).

9.2 Avoidance Conditioning

Skinner proposed that "avoidance conditioning" is "reinforced by escape from the shock." Mowrer and Miller suggested that "avoidance is reinforced by reduction in a CS-elicited fear drive" (LeDoux, 2014).

9.3 Fear Extinction

Adaptive behavior is characterized by "the use of past experience to guide future learning." According to the Rescorla-Wagner model, learning occurs when there is discrepancy between an expected and actual outcome. "In the case of fear learning, this is the discrepancy between the aversive unconditioned stimulus (US) that is actually delivered and the US that is expected based on prior conditioned stimulus (CS)–US pairings. Learning occurs preferentially to surprising outcomes and their antecedents at the expense of expected ones. When the expectation matches the outcome (i.e., there is no prediction error), no learning occurs" (Furlong et al., 2010). Adaptive behavior implies the ability to quickly and effectively replace existing association with new ones based on feedback. Failure to do so is linked to "a wide range of behavioral abnormalities or psychiatric conditions" (i.e., psychopathy; bipolar disorder; reactive aggression and severe conduct disorder) (Xue et al., 2013). Researchers have established that dopamine plays a vital role in reward-based learning and its expression. It has been proposed that "reward-related processes that rely on dopamine may drive the learning of extinction contingencies…During extinction, the fear response is suppressed as the organism learns that the CS no longer predicts the shock" (Abraham et al., 2014).

Discussion

From the educational (i.e., test anxiety; fear appeals) and health systems (i.e., fear appeals) through the judicial (i.e., prison staff using fear of sexual abuse to control inmates) and military sectors (i.e., fear experienced by children of war), fear represents a predominant emotion cultivated in humanity. Its effectiveness in extinguishing spirituality and contributing to the acquisition of absolute corporate profit explains why "fear learning mechanisms" are "one of the most intensely studied questions in neuroscience" while research on spirituality-based topics and topics exposing the crimes committed by governments and corporations is scarce, resisted and ignored.

References

Abraham, A. D., Neve, K. A. & Lattal, K. M. (2014). Dopamine and extinction: A convergence of theory with fear and reward circuitry. *Neurobiology of Learning and Memory*, *108*, 65-77.

Chou, D., Huang, C.-C. & Hsu, K.-S. (2014). Brain-derived neurotrophic factor in the amygdala mediates susceptibility to fear conditioning. *Experimental Neurology*, *255*, 19-29.

Field, A. P. & Schorah, H. (2007). The verbal information pathway to fear and heart rate changes in children. *Journal of Child Psychology and Psychiatry*, *48*(11), 1088-1093.

Furlong, T. M., Cole, S., Hamlin, A. S. & McNally, G. P. (2010). The role of prefrontal cortex in predictive fear learning. *Behavioral Neuroscience*, *124*(5), 574-586.

Duvarci, S. & Pare, D. (2014). Amygdala microcircuits controlling learned fear. *Neuron*, *82*, 966-980.

Gartstein, M. A., Bridgett, D. J., Rothbart, M. K., Robertson, C., Iddins, E., Ramsay, K. & Schlect, S. (2010). A latent growth examination of fear development in infancy: Contributions of maternal depression and the risk for toddler anxiety. *Developmental Psychology*, *46*(3), 651-668.

King, E. C., Pattwell, S. S., Sun, A., Glatt, C. E. & Lee, F. S. (2013). Nonlinear developmental trajectory of fear learning and memory. *Annals of the New York Academy of Sciences*, *1304*, 62-69.

Kong, E., Monje, F. J., Hirsch, J. & Pollak, D. D. (2014). Learning not to fear: Neural correlates of learned safety. *Neuropsychopharmacology*, *39*, 515–527.

LeDoux, J. E. (2014). Coming to terms with fear. *PNAS*, *111*(8), 2871-2878.

Rodebaugha, T. L., Weeks, J. W., Gordon, E. A., Langer, J. K. & Heimberg, R. G. (2012). The longitudinal relationship between fear of positive evaluation and fear of negative evaluation. *Anxiety, Stress, & Coping*, *25*(2), 167-182.

Schultz, D. H. & Helmstetter, F. J. (2010). Classical conditioning of autonomic fear responses is independent of contingency awareness. *Journal of Experimental Psychology: Animal Behavior Processes*, *36*(4), 495-500.

Xue, G., Xue, F., Droutman, V., Lu, Z.-L., Bechara, A. & Read, S. (2013). Common neural mechanisms underlying reversal learning by reward and punishment. *PLOS One*, *8*(12), 1-11.

Chapter 10

DIS-EASE

"The internal state of the body influences our perceptions, cognitions, and emotions" (Garfinkel et al., 2014).

**

"In Jungian terms, what has manifested as dis-ease in the person is psyche's attempt to self regulate and achieve psychic harmony. This occurs when one's internal suffering manifests in a physical, emotional or mental illness…the dis-eased self is in essence revealing an unconscious problem in a symbolic form that is somatized because it has no other way to express itself" (McClary, 2007). "Symbols mediate between the unrepresentable archetypes and the world of the manifest. They link the dark realm of indefinite power, vitality, and mystery to the well-lit world of ego consciousness with its relatively fixed meanings and limitations…A symbol can be amplified by an extended net of personal, cultural, and historical associations, but it can never be fully objectified and comprehended since its roots are in the unrepresentable archetype, in the most secret depths of the soul" (Mansfield, 1991).

10.1 Psychopathy

Psychopathy is a personality disorder. Lack of authenticity (Kimonis et al., 2012) which "involves creation and construction as well as discovery, originality and frequent opposition to the rules of society (even potentially to what we recognise as morality)" (Malm, 2008), lack of truthfulness, shame or remorse, pathologic egocentricity and insincere charm are traits characterizing psychopathy. There are two psychopathy variants. The primary variant is characterized by "a general lack of emotion and anxiety" while the secondary – by emotional reactivity resulting from increased levels of anxiety. Developmental precursors of psychopathy have been identified in childhood and adolescence whereas secondary psychopathy variant develops through environmental conditions such as competitive disadvantage, childhood neglect, abuse and trauma. "Karpman (1948) proposed that childhood abuse resulted in hostility that 'disturbed the functioning of an otherwise intact conscience.'" The research paradigm suggesting that childhood abuse and trauma precede secondary psychopathy is evidenced in the high rates of childhood insults experienced by incarcerated youth and adults (Kimonis et al., 2012).

10.2 Meditation and Imagery

"Mindfulness-based meditation interventions have become increasingly popular in contemporary psychology." Mindfulness-based therapy (MBT) has been shown to reduce negative psychological experiences (i.e. stress, anxiety, depression)." Loving-kindness meditation (LKM) and compassion meditation (CM) "are associated with an increase in positive affect and a decrease in negative affect" (Hofmann et al., 2011). Positive mental imagery practice exerts therapeutic effect on depression, a "debilitating" and frequently occurring disorder (Williams et al., 2013).

Discussion

Aggression and School Violence (2.24) suggested that prevention of "violent and undesirable behaviors" involves the capacity to "deal with the underlying causes of these behaviors." *Trafficking (6.7)* further proposed that prevention of human trafficking is embedded within "addressing root causes." Thus, similarly to the "'critical need for treatments' designed to prevent or diminish" the induced by the system at large "crimes committed by serious youth offenders" (*Juvenile Justice System, 7.1*), corporate and governing officials projecting a deeply dis-eased self onto the world require healing (i.e., meditation and imagery), not the spotlight.

References

Garfinkel, S. N., Minati, L., Gray, M. A., Seth, A. K., Dolan, R. J., Critchley, H. D. (2014). Fear from the heart: Sensitivity to fear stimuli depends on individual heartbeats. *The Journal of Neuroscience, 34*(19), 6573-6582.

Hofmann, S. G., Grossman, P. & Hinton, D. E. (2011). Loving-kindness and compassion meditation: Potential for psychological interventions. *Clinical Psychology Review, 31*(7), 1126-1132.

Kimonis, E. R., Tatar, J. R. & Cuffman, E. (2012). Substance-related disorders among juvenile offenders: What role do psychopathic traits play? *Psychology of Addictive Behaviors, 26*(2), 212-225.

Malm, B. (2008). Authenticity in teachers' lives and work: Some philosophical and empirical considerations. *Scandinavian Journal of Educational Research, 52*(4), 373-386.

Mansfield, V. (1991). The opposites in quantum physics and Jungian psychology: Part II: Applications. *Journal of Analytical Psychology, 36*, 289-306.

McClary, R. (2007). Healing the psyche through music, myth, and ritual. *Psychology of Aesthetics, Creativity, and the Arts, 1*(3), 155-159.

Williams, A.D., Blackwell, S. E., Mackenzie, A., Holmes, E. A. & Andrews, G. (2013). Combining imagination and reason in the treatment of depression: A randomized controlled trial of internet-based cognitive-bias modification and internet-CBT for depression. *Journal of Consulting and Clinical Psychology, 81*(5), 793-799.

Conclusion

"Underneath our political, social, and economic arrangements, the way modern culture defines and understands reality itself is faulty, and this flawed way of knowing gives rise to distorted, we might even say cancerous, forms of technology and economic organization" (Miller, 2001). Technological and economic advances are neither the driving forces nor the guarantee of human progress (Vayalilkarottu, 2012). Profit and power alone do not result in personal fulfillment (Miller, 2001). A growing body of research "asserts that materialism, the pursuit of worldly possessions and wealth, does not give lasting happiness and fulfillment. Instead, it increases people's dissatisfaction, depression, anxiety, anger, isolation and alienation (Vayalilkarottu, 2012). The absolute focus on "comforts and luxuries," whether acquired honestly or "at the expense of other people and other living beings," is evaluated by mythology, religious tradition and much of our prominent dramatic literature as "morally inadequate, psychologically deficient, or explicitly subhuman" (Miller, 2001).

If spirituality is innate and the global governing system is cultivating the exact opposite to spirituality environment for self-serving purposes, it is not humanity that needs to change to reflect the corporate agenda. Rather, starting with education, the global system of governance requires transformation to reflect spirituality. It is critical that "we extract ourselves from the current paradigm and move from 'miseducation to mindful education'" (*Standardization, 2.3.2*) for "if the search for truth is discarded from the purposes of human learning... the integrity of learning... is lost" (*Emotional Intelligence, 2.10*).

Freedom signifies "our ability to intervene between stimulus and response so that we will not simply keep responding automatically to situations in which we find ourselves" (*Premises, 4.2*). Scholars "possess the access, resources and theoretical background necessary to challenge the 'taken-for-granted notions of managerial discourse'" thus "preserving the original goal of the university – to allow for understanding of the world and 'the development of human potential'" (*Mainstream Education*). "The new role of the teacher is to become a moral philosopher" (*Spiritual Intelligence, 2.11*) and to focus on the "good points of each child" and not on his or her weaknesses ((*Premises, 4.2*) for "children are the revolutionary bridge, continuously rebuilding the connection between present and future states of planet Earth" *(Earth, 2.31)*.

References

Miller, R. (2001). Making connections to the world some thoughts on holistic curriculum. *ENCOUNTER: Education for Meaning and Social Justice, 14*(4), 29-35.

Vayalilkarottu, J. (2012). Holistic health and well-being: A psycho-spiritual/religious and theological perspective. *Asian Journal of Psychiatry, 5*, 347-350.

About the Authors

Sosé Gjelaj was born in Montenegro. She relocated to the United States with her family in 1969 and has lived in America since then. Sosé is an author, a philanthropist, a published poet and a pronoun artist who had spent a lifetime studying Eastern and Western philosophy. She has academic background in Arts and is the owner of "Sosé Art Gallery" located in Bennington, VT. Sosé is the founder of the "Source of Visibility," a not-for-profit humanitarian and environmental organization.

Elitsa Teneva was born in Bulgaria. She moved to the United States when she was 18 to pursue an academic career in the fields of psychology and school psychology. She graduated with a B.S. in Psychology and a minor in Child Development from Southern Vermont College in Bennington, VT, and M.Ed. with a concentration in School Psychology from the University of Massachusetts Amherst, Amherst, MA. Elitsa is a member on the Board of Directors of the "Source of Visibility."

Other Books by the Authors

SOVEREIGN TERRA by Sosé Gjelaj and Elitsa Teneva

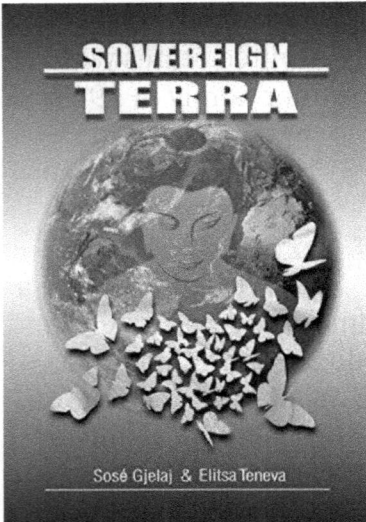

Based on a theory devised by Sosé Gjelaj and with the support of 445 peer-reviewed scientific articles, "Sovereign Terra" takes a revolutionary perspective on the state of humanity and the environment and the root cause of human disease and environmental degradation. Human and environmental deterioration are the product of a secretive agenda designed by governmental and industrial enterprises to acquire absolute profit and power at the expense of human life and environmental wellness. While humanity is deceived to believe that all care is taken by key officials to ameliorate the ever-accelerating human and environmental destruction, in truth, all planning and action is undertaken to destruct the human race and Earth. Humanity and Earth are on the verge of grand-scale collapse whether manifested through environmental disaster, human disease outbreaks or the combination of both.

We can no longer depend on those we elect to save us and our environment if we are to thrive and ensure that future generations breathe fresh air, drink clean water and consume food free of chemicals. We must act now and take full responsibility for ourselves and our planetary home. The longer we delay the implementation of restorative interventions, the more severely we will experience the devastating consequences of escalating deterioration. The first step to healing ourselves and Earth is awareness, the grand awakening to the truth. "Sovereign Terra" opens the eyes to the visibly invisible so we can, individually and collectively, consciously take action, save ourselves and Earth.

SYNCHRONIZATION OF DIMENSIONS by Sosé Gjelaj and Elitsa Teneva

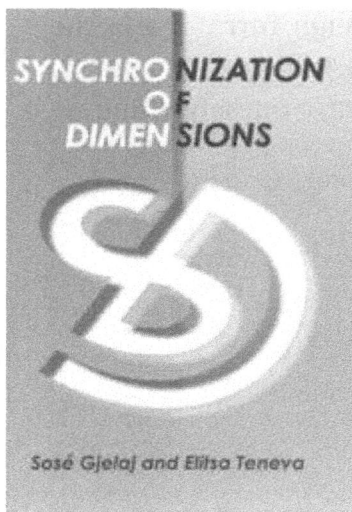

Synchronization of Dimensions takes us on a journey of the deepest questions and answers facing mankind today. Topics such as human and universally created laws, sexual energy and the difference between darkness and light are a few of the topics explored. Delving into the magic of wisdom, the reader is left with a clear understanding of his origins, spiritual makeup and genetic future.

THE 13ᵀᴴ SECRET CODE by Sosé Gjelaj

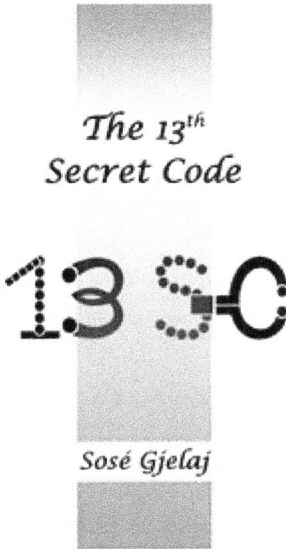

The 13ᵗʰ
Secret Code

13 SC

Sosé Gjelaj

The 13th Secret Code is a compilation of selected poems written by Sosé Gjelaj in the past almost five decades. Sosé's wisdom and creativity flow through the pages as the reader delves into the ocean of source energy and the experiences of our eternal soul. Love, the evolution of human consciousness and the unknown are some of the topics that Sosé explores through her artistic pen. The reader is gifted with a masterpiece of mystery and magic.

www.ingramcontent.com/pod-product-compliance
Lightning Source LLC
Chambersburg PA
CBHW062213080426
42734CB00010B/1878